D0578313

The Love of
Chinese
Cooking

The Love of
Chinese
Cooking

Kenneth Lo

OCTOPUS

Contents

First published 1977 by
Octopus Books Limited
59 Grosvenor Street
London W1

© 1977 Octopus Books Limited

ISBN 0 7064 0593 5

Produced by Mandarin Publishers Limited
22a Westlands Road
Quarry Bay, Hong Kong
Printed in Hong Kong

Introduction

It is surprisingly easy to cook Chinese food in a western kitchen. Contrary to myth, a whole collection of exotic cooking utensils is not necessary and, in fact, nothing very fancy in the way of western equipment is required either — just a few good quality, heavy-based saucepans, frying-pans and perhaps a flameproof casserole. Nearly all the foods used in Chinese cooking will be familiar too: rice, flour, pasta, meat, poultry, fish, shellfish, vegetables and fruit. Even the prime flavourings are much the same: salt, pepper, sugar, vinegar, wine, etc. And, as to actual cooking techniques, the most popular are roasting, boiling, deep-frying, shallow-frying, steaming, grilling (broiling) and barbecuing — none of them exactly unknown to the western cook. The only important technique not so familiar in the west is quick stir-frying, but once the concept of this is grasped, its simplicity will more than outweigh its newness.

Where there is a difference, it is in emphasis and approach to the use of foods, seasonings, flavourings and especially in heating and cooking. For instance, Chinese soups (which are traditionally drunk throughout the meal), are usually clear consommés in which a host of materials may be cooked, both quickly and at length, to produce some specially desired flavour. Vegetable dishes are frequently cooked for such short periods of time that they are rather like hot salads and, if more lengthily cooked, as in the case of hard or semi-hard vegetables, they are more often cooked in their own juice than in large quantities of water. Meat dishes are either cooked more slowly than in the west (for tenderness and richness of flavour), or much more quickly (for freshness and crispiness). Perhaps there is a more conscious and deliberate use of flavoured oils (strong-tasting vegetables, such as ginger, garlic, onion, chilli pepper, salt and salted black beans are often cooked for a short time in a small amount of oil to impart to the latter a flavour), which are in turn used to cook the main ingredients. Flavoured fat is also used to make vegetables and pasta more succulent and appealing. Apart from soya sauce, a whole range of soya bean products are used as seasonings and flavourings to produce a whole range of tastes particular to Chinese food: soya bean paste, soya bean jam, soya bean-curd cheese, salted black beans and hoisin sauce (a mixture of soya beans and vegetable extracts).

The rest is in the cooking, and particularly in the control of heat during the cooking period. The Chinese seem to have a much greater regard for finesse in the matter of 'heat control' or 'fire power' than westerners, and it is this control which characterizes the great Chinese chefs, who 'conduct' heat in much the same way as an accomplished conductor conducts music — from the hand. Chinese chefs appreciate that great heat suddenly applied will not only seal in the natural juices (of food being cooked in small or thin pieces), but also cook the food through in a very short time without allowing the juices to escape — thus leaving the end product more succulent. At the same time, they appreciate that when cooking tough foods it is better to rely on a long sustained cooking time than on any intense short burst of heat; for when low heat is used to cook tough food without drowning it in water, a high degree of tenderness can be achieved without the material becoming fibrous and thereby causing the flavour to disperse into the cooking liquid.

Although some forty Chinese cooking and heating methods could be said to exist, in point of fact there are only relatively few methods which anyone really needs to know in order to start to cook Chinese food. They are as follows:

Quick stir-frying

This is the method which, to most westerners, denotes Chinese cooking. It consists of heating a small amount of oil and fat over moderate to high heat (mostly the latter) and adding to it in turn various ingredients which are to be cooked — those requiring longer cooking first, those which require only very short cooking last — and then stirring and turning in the hot oil, at first individually then all together, either leisurely or at speed. Vegetables, meats (usually the tender cuts like fillet), poultry and fish may be marinated or seasoned before being added to the pan, or the seasonings and flavourings may be added during the course of cooking. Often the cooking oil or fat used may itself be flavoured first by cooking and stirring in dried, seasoned or strongly-flavoured ingredients. By varying the heat employed and the seasonings and flavourings used, as well as the ingredients to be incorporated, the number of dishes which can be prepared by quick stir-frying is practically unlimited. As the time required for this method of cooking is extremely short (1–3 minutes), it is a style of cooking which is much favoured by restaurants. But it is a method of cooking which is labour-intensive for the food to be cooked, both main and supplementary, must be reduced to uniform thin slices, small cubes or shreds or threads before cooking can start. One of the most important things to remember when practising quick stir-frying is not to pile up the ingredients in the pan, one on top of the other, otherwise they will begin to 'sweat', which will result in the food being stewed and limp rather than fried and crisp. Quick stir-frying must also, above all, be *quick.* The oil or fat must be really hot before the first ingredients are added, and the next lot should be added only when the first batch is quickly cooked through. The general stirring, turning and scrambling together, with the addition of the final phase of flavourings, should proceed only when all the ingredients in the pan are sizzling hot. The majority of quick stir-fried dishes should be consumed as soon as possible after they leave the pan, for connoisseurs consider the 'heat' to be an essential part of the flavour.

Red-cooking

Red-cooking is a form of stewing, with soya sauce. But it is stewing with a difference, for much less water is used (sometimes none at all), and fewer vegetables are added. Ingredients which are incorporated right from the start are usually dried, pickled or salted. The temperature is kept deliberately very low (after first bringing the contents to a boil), and this low temperature is maintained throughout a comparatively long period of time (1¼ to 3½ hours, depending on the meat or fish being cooked). The action of the soya sauce, together with one or two other ingredients such as a small amount of sugar and wine, causes the main meat of the dish to become extremely tender and succulent. Most meat and poultry can be cooked very successfully by red-cooking and, unlike quick stir-frying, it is a method of cooking which is not labour intensive. Most red-cooked dishes will also keep well for a few days in the refrigerator, and they are just as good re-heated as they are when first cooked.

Clear-simmering

Clear-simmering is another slow cooking process, but one in which no soya sauce is used. The cooking is usually done in clear broth (or water) where, by keeping the temperature deliberately low (after bringing to an initial boil), the broth or soup keeps meticulously clear throughout cooking. The aim of this method is to achieve great tenderness and purity of the food being cooked (usually meat or poultry). The flavour of the broth is usually enhanced by the use of a small amount of pickled, dried or salted ingredients, added at the beginning of the cooking period, and the introduction of a few or a range of tender fresh food and vegetables during the concluding stages. Meat cooked in this way is generally tender enough to be pulled apart with a pair of chopsticks, and is traditionally dipped in some type of soya-dip before eating. It is also traditional to serve the cooking liquid as a clear soup, along with the vegetables which should still be fresh and crisp. Clear-simmering dishes probably correspond to some of the great 'boiled' dishes of mediaeval European cooking.

Steaming

There are two types of steaming in China: closed steaming and open steaming. Closed steaming is very similar to clear-simmering already explained, and is a process of slow cooking where a receptacle containing the food to be cooked is placed inside a steamer and steamed for several hours over steady, even heat, so that the finished food will achieve a high degree of tenderness. Physically it is much like cooking in a double-boiler. Open steaming is a quick process of cooking, where the food to be cooked is placed on a heatproof dish with all the attendant supplementary materials, seasonings and flavourings added, and steamed vigorously for a short period of time (5–20 minutes). The aim is to produce a 'pure' dish where the food and shape of the finished dish are not unduly disturbed by the cooking process. The dish should, in fact, appear much the same cooked as when it is uncooked. Only very fresh food can be cooked in this manner, and there is no better way. Fish and seafood are often cooked by open steaming. One advantage of steaming over other forms of cooking is that all the ingredients can be pre-arranged and pre-dressed on the serving dish before cooking commences.

Quick-roasting

This is a method of roasting (called Cha Shao) meat or poultry, which are first of all seasoned and marinated, at a high temperature for a short time (10–15 minutes). When subjected to sudden high temperature the seasonings and marinade are often encrusted on to the surface of the meat, forming a highly seasoned and savoury layer, which contrasts well with the fresh, natural flavour of the inside of the meat (not unlike a charcoal grilled [broiled] Châteaubriand steak). This is a method of cooking particularly adaptable to western tastes and practices, and it is particularly good when entertaining; the dish can be marinated and otherwise prepared for cooking long before it needs to be cooked and served, and the actual cooking is simple to do. Only really good quality, tender meat is suitable for this type of cooking — fillet (tenderloin) or pork is the cut most usually cooked in this way.

Chinese ingredients

Although the Chinese use a wide range of flavourings, in the form of sauces, dried, salted and pickled food and strong-tasting vegetables, the following are those most frequently used. They are of course normally used in conjunction with more familiar ingredients.

Sauces
Soya sauce
Soya paste (salty)
Soya jam (sweet)
Bean-curd 'cheese' (red or cream coloured)
Hoisin sauce
Oyster sauce
Shrimp sauce (or paste)
Fish sauce
Plum sauce

Dried Foods
Dried mushrooms
Dried salted black beans
Dried chilli peppers (hot)
Dried wood ears (black fungi)
Dried shrimps
Dried scallops
Dried squid
Five spice powder (also sold in mixed pieces) — a combination of star anise, anise pepper, fennel, cloves and cinnamon. Should be used sparingly in powder form.
Beche-de-mer (or sea cucumber)

Pickled Vegetables
Snow pickles or hseuh tsai (salted pickled greens sold in cans)
Winter pickles or tientsin tung tsai (flaky cream-coloured pickled vegetables sold in jars)

Strong-Tasting Vegetables
Root ginger (gnarled potato-like root)
Garlic
Spring onion (scallion)

The recipes in this book are enough for two people with good appetites, three people with average appetites or four people with small appetites, unless otherwise stated.

TIBET

BAY OF BENGAL

REGIONS OF CHINA

MONGOLIA

SEA OF JAPAN

The Great Wall

PEKING

Hwang Ho

YELLOW SEA

Sian

Nanking

SHANGHAI

Wuhan

EAST CHINA SEA

SZECHUAN

Yangtze · Chunking

FUKIEN

Si Kiang · CANTON

HONG KONG

SOUTH CHINA SEA

One-dish meals

The dishes in this first chapter have been specially selected for the ease with which they can be cooked, and for the fact that, with rice, they constitute an entire meal. They run the gamut of all of the main cooking techniques, from quick-fried dishes to red-cooked, to the popular southern Chinese cha shao, or quick-roasting. Except in the quick-fried dishes where, in the majority of cases, the meat and vegetable ingredients are mixed together during cooking, the vegetables are usually prepared simply and separately. In red-cooking and quick roasting in particular, it is the meat part of the 'combination' which should provide the gravy or sauce, which is essential in making the rice palatable. And in each case where the vegetable is cooked separately, it is done simply (quick-fried and braised in clear broth with some oil, fat or butter) without much use of soya sauce. In all of the dishes in this chapter, rice forms the main bulk food. So to each of these one-platter dishes there are three aspects: the plain cooked rice which should form the bed or base of the dish; the rich, brown-coloured meat with gravy; and the fresh light-coloured (or green) vegetables. In quick-fried dishes, where the meat and vegetables are cooked together, the complete dish is usually even more colourful, as often more than one vegetable is incorporated, and crisply and quickly cooked with the meat.

Since rice forms the base of all of the dishes which follow, the chapter starts off with a simple method of cooking it.

Boiled rice

Boiled rice should be fairly dry and flaky.

Place 450g/1lb (2⅔ cups) of raw long-grain rice in a heavy-based saucepan. Rinse once or twice under cold running water, then drain off the water. Add about 1¼ times (about 550ml/18 fl oz (2¼ cups) of its own equivalent in volume of fresh water. Bring to the boil, cover with a well-fitting lid and place an asbestos sheet under the pan. After 1 minute, reduce the heat to very low and simmer very gently for 10 minutes. Turn the heat off altogether and leave the rice to cook in its own heat for 10–12 minutes. It should then be ready to serve.

Rice cooked in this way should be used in all the dishes which follow.

Quick-fried chicken with mushrooms and peas

METRIC/IMPERIAL	AMERICAN
2 boned chicken breasts, each weighing about 225 g/½lb	2 boned chicken breasts, each weighing about ½lb
60 ml/4 tbsp vegetable oil	4 tbsp vegetable oil
5 ml/1 tsp salt	1 tsp salt
pepper	pepper
8 medium-sized mushrooms	8 medium-sized mushrooms
30 ml/2 tbsp butter	2 tbsp butter
225 g/½lb peas (shelled weight)	1 cup peas (shelled weight)
5 ml/1 tsp sugar	1 tsp sugar
30 ml/2 tbsp soya sauce	2 tbsp soy sauce
½ chicken stock cube	½ chicken stock cube
45 ml/3 tbsp water or clear broth (page 25)	3 tbsp water or clear broth (page 25)
450 g/1lb cooked rice	6 cups cooked rice

To prepare: Cut the chicken into cubes. Rub all over with a quarter of the oil and sprinkle with salt and pepper. Remove the stalks from the mushrooms and chop stalks and caps separately.

To cook: Heat the remaining oil and the butter in a large frying-pan over high heat. When the fat has melted, add the mushroom stalks. Stir-fry for 1 minute. Add the diced chicken cubes and stir-fry for 1 minute. Add the peas and remaining mushrooms. Sprinkle with the sugar, soya sauce, crumbled stock cube and water or broth. Stir-fry for 2 minutes.

To serve: Arrange the cooked rice on a warmed platter and spoon over the chicken mixture.

Quick-fried pork in sweet and sour sauce with peppers and tomatoes

METRIC/IMPERIAL	AMERICAN
450 g/1lb lean boned leg of pork	1lb lean boned leg of pork
15 ml/1 tbsp flour	1 tbsp flour
5 ml/1 tsp salt	1 tsp salt
1 medium-sized green pepper	1 medium-sized green pepper
3 medium-sized tomatoes	3 medium-sized tomatoes
60 ml/4 tbsp vegetable oil	4 tbsp vegetable oil
450 g/1lb cooked rice	6 cups cooked rice

Sauce	Sauce
20 ml/1¼ tbsp sugar	1¼ tbsp sugar
30 ml/2 tbsp white wine vinegar	2 tbsp white wine vinegar
15 ml/1 tbsp tomato purée	1 tbsp tomato paste
45 ml/3 tbsp orange juice	3 tbsp orange juice
15 ml/1 tbsp soya sauce	1 tbsp soy sauce
15 ml/1 tbsp cornflour, mixed with 60 ml/4 tbsp water	1 tbsp cornstarch, mixed with 4 tbsp water

To prepare: Cut the pork into cubes. Rub all over with the flour and sprinkle with salt. Remove the pith and seeds from the pepper and cut into small pieces. Cut the tomatoes into quarters. Combine all the sauce ingredients until they are well blended.

To cook: Heat the oil in a large frying-pan over high heat. When the oil is very hot, add the pork cubes. Stir-fry for 2½ minutes. Add the pepper and tomatoes and stir-fry for 1 minute. Pour in the sauce and gently toss and turn the ingredients in it until they are well coated. Cook for a few seconds more, until the sauce thickens.

To serve: Arrange the cooked rice on a warmed platter and spoon over the pork mixture.

Quick-fried beef with tomatoes and peas

METRIC/IMPERIAL	AMERICAN
450 g/1lb fillet or rump of beef	1lb fillet or rump of beef
60 ml/4 tbsp vegetable oil	4 tbsp vegetable oil
5 ml/1 tsp salt	1 tsp salt
pepper	pepper
2 medium-sized onions	2 medium-sized onions
2 spring onions	2 scallions
2–3 tomatoes	2–3 tomatoes
30 ml/2 tbsp butter	2 tbsp butter
225 g/½lb peas (shelled weight)	1 cup peas (shelled weight)
5 ml/1 tsp sugar	1 tsp sugar
30 ml/2 tbsp soya sauce	2 tbsp soy sauce
½ chicken stock cube	½ chicken stock cube
60 ml/4 tbsp water	4 tbsp water
15 ml/1 tbsp cornflour, mixed with 60 ml/4 tbsp water	1 tbsp cornstarch, mixed with 4 tbsp water
450 g/1lb cooked rice	6 cups cooked rice

To prepare: Cut the beef into cubes. Rub all over with a quarter of the oil and sprinkle with salt and pepper. Slice the onions thinly and cut the spring onions (scallions) into 1.5 cm/½in lengths. Cut tomatoes into quarters.

To cook: Heat the remaining oil and the butter in a large frying-pan over high heat. When the fat has melted, add the onions. Stir-fry for 1 minute. Push the onions to the sides of the pan. Add the beef cubes and stir-fry for 1 minute. Add the spring onions (scallions), peas and tomatoes. Sprinkle with sugar, soya sauce, crumbled stock cube and water. Stir until the ingredients are well blended, and bring to the boil. Pour over the cornflour (cornstarch) mixture and stir until the sauce thickens.

To serve: Arrange the cooked rice on a warmed platter and spoon over the beef mixture.

Quick-fried beef with tomatoes and peas

Quick-fried lamb with leeks

METRIC/IMPERIAL	AMERICAN
450 g/1lb boned leg of lamb	1lb boned leg of lamb
60 ml/4 tbsp vegetable oil	4 tbsp vegetable oil
5 ml/1 tsp salt	1 tsp salt
pepper	pepper
2 small leeks	2 small leeks
2–3 slices root ginger (optional)	2–3 slices root ginger (optional)
15 ml/1 tbsp butter	1 tbsp butter
7.5 ml/1½ tsp sugar	1½ tsp sugar
30 ml/2 tbsp soya sauce	2 tbsp soy sauce
15 ml/1 tbsp cornflour, mixed with 60 ml/4 tbsp water	1 tbsp cornstarch, mixed with 4 tbsp water
15 ml/1 tbsp dry sherry	1 tbsp dry sherry
450 g/1lb hot cooked rice (page 12)	6 cups hot cooked rice (page 12)

To prepare: Slice the lamb thinly, then cut into 2.5 cm/1 in pieces. Rub all over with a quarter of the oil and sprinkle with salt and pepper. Clean the leeks thoroughly and cut into 1.5 cm/½ in lengths. Peel and grate the ginger.

To cook: Heat the remaining oil in a large frying-pan over high heat. When the oil is very hot, add the lamb slices and ginger. Stir and turn a few times, then push them to one side of the pan. Melt the butter in the pan and add the leeks. Stir and turn a few times. Add the sugar and soya sauce and stir-fry the lamb and leeks separately for ¾ minute. Pour the cornflour (cornstarch) mixture over the lamb and the sherry over the leeks. Mix the two sets of ingredients together for ¼ minute.

To serve: Arrange the cooked rice on a warmed platter and spoon over the lamb mixture.

Quick-fried pork with bean sprouts and spring onions (scallions)

METRIC/IMPERIAL	AMERICAN
450 g/1lb lean pork	1lb lean pork
30 ml/2 tbsp soya sauce	2 tbsp soy sauce
60 ml/4 tbsp vegetable oil	4 tbsp vegetable oil
5 ml/1 tsp salt	1 tsp salt
4 spring onions	4 scallions
25 ml/1½ tbsp butter	1½ tbsp butter
350 g/¾ lb bean sprouts	2 cups bean sprouts
5 ml/1 tsp sugar	1 tsp sugar
30 ml/2 tbsp boiling water	2 tbsp boiling water
25 ml/1½ tbsp dry sherry	1½ tbsp dry sherry
450 g/1lb hot cooked rice (page 12)	6 cups hot cooked rice (page 12)

To prepare: Slice the pork thinly, then cut into 2.5 cm/1 in pieces. Rub all over with half the soya sauce and quarter of the

Quick-fried pork with bean sprouts and spring onions (scallions)

oil. Sprinkle with salt. Cut the spring onions (scallions) into 2.5 cm/1 in lengths.

To cook: Heat the remaining oil in a large frying-pan over high heat. When the oil is hot, add the pork slices. Stir-fry for 2¼ minutes, then remove from the pan. Melt the butter in the pan and add the bean sprouts and spring onions (scallions). Stir-fry for 1 minute. Sprinkle with the remaining soya sauce, the sugar and water. Stir-fry for ½ minute. Return the pork to the pan. Add the sherry and stir-fry for a further 1 minute.

To serve: Arrange the cooked rice on a warmed platter and spoon over the pork mixture.

Quick-fried prawns (shrimps) with bacon, mushrooms and cucumber

METRIC/IMPERIAL	AMERICAN
2 cloves garlic	*2 cloves garlic*
2 slices root ginger (optional)	*2 slices root ginger (optional)*
350–450 g/¾–1lb prawns (shelled weight)	*¾–1lb shrimps (shelled weight)*
60 ml/4 tbsp vegetable oil	*4 tbsp vegetable oil*
5 ml/1 tsp salt	*1 tsp salt*
pepper	*pepper*
1 medium-sized onion	*1 medium-sized onion*
	2–3 slices fatty bacon
2–3 rashers streaky bacon	*1½–2 cups mushrooms*
225–350 g/½–¾ lb mushrooms	*½ medium-sized cucumber*
½ medium-sized cucumber	*1 tbsp butter*
15 ml/1 tbsp butter	*1 tsp sugar*
5 ml/1 tsp sugar	*1½ tbsp soy sauce*
25 ml/1½ tbsp soya sauce	*2 tbsp dry sherry*
30 ml/2 tbsp dry sherry	*6 cups hot cooked rice (page 12)*
450 g/1lb hot cooked rice (page 12)	

To prepare: Crush the garlic, then peel and chop the ginger into small pieces. Rub the prawns (shrimps) all over with the garlic, ginger and a quarter of the oil. Sprinkle with salt and pepper. Slice the onion thinly. Cut the bacon, crosswise, into thin strips. Remove and discard the stalks from the mushrooms, then chop the caps. Chop the cucumber into 1.5 cm/½ in cubes.

To cook: Heat the remaining oil and the butter in a large frying-pan over high heat. When the fat has melted, add the onion. Stir-fry for ½ minute. Add the mushrooms and bacon and stir-fry for 1 minute. Add the prawns (shrimps) and cucumber and sprinkle over the sugar and soya sauce. Stir-fry for 2 minutes. Stir in the sherry and cook for a few seconds more.

To serve: Arrange the cooked rice on a warmed platter and spoon over the prawn (shrimp) mixture.

Quick-fried prawns (shrimps) with bacon, mushrooms and cucumber

Cha shao quick-roast pork with cabbage

The drippings from the meat in this dish can be used to make gravy, or for cooking accompanying vegetables. Only the best cuts of meat should be used in this type of cooking.

METRIC/IMPERIAL	AMERICAN
700 g/1 ½ lb pork fillet	*1 ½ lb pork tenderloin*
1 small cabbage	*1 small cabbage*
15 ml/1 tbsp butter	*1 tbsp butter*
½ chicken stock cube	*½ chicken stock cube*
15 ml/1 tbsp soya sauce	*1 tbsp soy sauce*
salt and pepper	*salt and pepper*
75–90 ml/5–6 tbsp water	*5–6 tbsp water*
450 g/1lb hot cooked rice (page 12)	*6 cups hot cooked rice (page 12)*

Marinade	**Marinade**
25 ml/1 ½ tbsp soya sauce	*1 ½ tbsp soy sauce*
15 ml/1 tbsp hoisin sauce or soya paste	*1 tbsp hoisin sauce or soy paste*
7.5 ml/1 ½ tsp soya jam (optional)	*1 ½ tsp soy jam (optional)*
2.5 ml/½ tsp salt	*½ tsp salt*
25 ml/1 ½ tbsp vegetable oil	*1 ½ tbsp vegetable oil*
7.5 ml/1 ½ tsp sugar	*1 ½ tsp sugar*

To prepare: Combine all the marinade ingredients until they are well blended. Add the pork and baste well. Leave for 2–2½ hours, turning the pork every 30 minutes. Shred the cabbage.
To cook: Arrange the pork on a rack in a roasting pan. Put into the oven preheated to 230–240°C (450–475°F) Gas Mark 8–9. Roast for 12–14 minutes, turning once. Remove the pork from the oven and keep hot. Put the roasting pan (with the drippings) over moderate heat and add the butter. When the fat has melted, add the cabbage. Stir and turn to coat well. Sprinkle with the crumbled stock cube, soya sauce, seasoning and water. Increase the heat to fairly high, cover and cook for 2–3 minutes, adding more water if necessary.
To serve: Cut the pork across the grain into thin slices. Arrange the cooked rice on a warmed platter and top with the pork, gravy and cabbage.

Cha shao quick-roast beef with leeks

METRIC/IMPERIAL	AMERICAN
Marinade (above)	*Marinade (above)*
700 g/1 ½ lb fillet of beef	*1 ½ lb fillet of beef*
2 slices root ginger	*2 slices root ginger*
3 leeks	*3 leeks*
25 ml/1 ½ tbsp butter	*1 ½ tbsp butter*
½ chicken stock cube	*½ chicken stock cube*
15 ml/1 tbsp soya sauce	*1 tbsp soy sauce*
75–90 ml/5–6 tbsp water	*5–6 tbsp water*
5 ml/1 tsp sugar	*1 tsp sugar*
450 g/1lb hot cooked rice (page 12)	*6 cups hot cooked rice (page 12)*

To prepare: Prepare the marinade. Cut the beef lengthways into two pieces. Peel and grate the ginger. Sprinkle the beef with the ginger, then add to the marinade and baste well. Leave for 1 hour. Clean leeks. Cut into 1.5 cm/½ in lengths.

To cook: Arrange the beef pieces on a rack in a roasting pan. Put into the oven preheated to 230–240°C (450–475°F) Gas Mark 8–9. Roast for 10–11 minutes, turning once. Remove the beef from the oven and keep hot. Put the roasting pan (with the drippings) over moderate heat and add the butter. When the fat has melted, add the leeks. Stir and turn to coat well. Sprinkle with the crumbled stock cube, soya sauce, water and sugar. Increase the heat to fairly high, cover and cook for 2 minutes, adding more water if necessary.
To serve: Cut each beef piece across the grain into 1.5 cm/½ in thick slices. Arrange the cooked rice on a warmed platter and top with the beef, gravy and leeks.

Red-cooked fish with onions and spring onions (scallions)

METRIC/IMPERIAL	AMERICAN
700 g/1 ½ lb fish, such as cod, haddock, turbot, carp, rock salmon, etc.	*1 ½ lb fish, such as cod, haddock, turbot, carp, rock salmon, etc.*
2–3 slices root ginger	*2–3 slices root ginger*
15 ml/1 tbsp flour	*1 tbsp flour*
5 ml/1 tsp salt	*1 tsp salt*
2 medium-sized onions	*2 medium-sized onions*
3 spring onions	*3 scallions*
55 ml/3 ½ tbsp soya sauce	*3 ½ tbsp soy sauce*
45 ml/3 tbs red wine or sherry	*3 tbsp red wine or sherry*
7.5 ml/1 ½ tsp sugar	*1 ½ tsp sugar*
75 ml/5 tbsp vegetable oil	*5 tbsp vegetable oil*
450 g/1lb hot cooked rice (page 12)	*6 cups hot cooked rice (page 12)*

To prepare: Cut the fish into 4 cm/1½ in pieces. Peel and grate the ginger. Rub all over with the flour, salt and ginger. Leave for 30 minutes. Slice the onions thinly. Cut the spring onions (scallions) into 2.5 cm/1in lengths. Combine the soya sauce, wine or sherry and sugar until they are well blended.
To cook: Heat 30 ml/2 tbsp of the oil in a frying-pan over moderate heat. When the oil is hot, add the onions. Stir-fry for 2 minutes. Push them to one side of the pan. Add the remaining oil to the pan. When it is hot, add the fish pieces and fry for 2 minutes on each side. Pour in the soya sauce mixture and toss and turn the fish pieces in it until they are well coated. Mix the onions into the sauce, then spoon over the fish. Sprinkle with the spring onions (scallions). Cover the pan and cook for 3–4 minutes.
To serve: Arrange the cooked rice on a warmed platter and spoon over the fish mixture.

Cha shao quick-roast pork with cabbage

Red-cooked chicken with cauliflower

This recipe is particularly recommended for reheating, so the quantities given below are enough for two meals for two people.

METRIC/IMPERIAL	AMERICAN
1 × 1½–2 kg/3–4 lb chicken	1 × 3–4 lb chicken
75–90 ml/5–6 tbsp soya sauce	5–6 tbsp soy sauce
150 ml/¼ pint water	⅝ cup water
12.5 ml/2½ tsp sugar	2½ tsp sugar
1 large cauliflower	1 large cauliflower
1½ chicken stock cubes	1½ chicken stock cubes
600 ml/1 pint hot stock	2½ cups hot stock
45 ml/3 tbsp vegetable oil	3 tbsp vegetable oil
60 ml/4 tbsp dry sherry	4 tbsp dry sherry
salt and pepper	salt and pepper
30 ml/2 tbsp butter	2 tbsp butter
450 g/1 lb hot cooked rice (page 12)	6 cups hot cooked rice (page 12)

To prepare: Cut or saw the chicken, through the bone, into 15–20 pieces. Combine the soya sauce, water and sugar until they are well blended. Divide the cauliflower into small flowerets. Dissolve the stock cubes in the stock.

To cook: Heat the oil in a flameproof casserole over moderate heat. When the oil is hot, add the chicken pieces. Stir-fry for 5–6 minutes. Pour in the soya mixture and toss the chicken pieces in it until they are well coated. Bring to the boil. Remove the casserole from the heat and cover. Put into the oven preheated to 140°C (275°F) Gas Mark 1. Cook for 1 hour, stirring once or twice. Stir in the sherry. Re-cover and return to the oven for a further 45 minutes, stirring once or twice. Meanwhile, pour the stock into a saucepan and bring to the boil. Add the cauliflower pieces and cook over fairly high heat for 2 minutes. Drain the cauliflower (the cooking broth can be reserved for future use), sprinkle with salt and pepper and toss in butter.

To serve: Arrange the cooked rice on a warmed platter and spoon over the chicken, gravy and cauliflower.

'Scrambled egg and bacon' with quick-fried peas and tomatoes

METRIC/IMPERIAL	AMERICAN
3–4 rashers streaky bacon	3–4 slices fatty bacon
4 eggs	4 eggs
5 ml/1 tsp salt	1 tsp salt
pepper	pepper
4–5 medium-sized tomatoes	4–5 medium-sized tomatoes
1 medium-sized onion	1 medium-sized onion
60 ml/4 tbsp vegetable oil	4 tbsp vegetable oil
25 ml/1½ tbsp butter	1½ tbsp butter
225 g/½ lb peas (shelled weight)	1 cup peas (shelled weight)
½ chicken stock cube	½ chicken stock cube
45 ml/3 tbsp boiling water	3 tbsp boiling water
25 ml/1½ tbsp soya sauce	1½ tbsp soy sauce
7.5 ml/1½ tsp sugar	1½ tsp sugar
450 g/1 lb hot cooked rice (page 12)	6 cups hot cooked rice (page 12)

To prepare: Cut the bacon, crosswise, into thin strips. Break the eggs into a bowl and sprinkle with salt and pepper. Beat

until they are well blended. Cut the tomatoes into quarters. Slice the onion thinly.

To cook: Heat the oil in a large frying-pan over high heat. When the oil is hot, add the onion and bacon. Stir-fry for 1 minute. Pour over the beaten eggs, tilting the pan so they spread out evenly. Cook without stirring for 1 minute. Remove from the heat and leave until the eggs are just about to

'Scrambled egg' and mixed vegetables with sweet and sour sauce

METRIC/IMPERIAL	AMERICAN
4–5 eggs	4–5 eggs
5 ml/1 tsp salt	1 tsp salt
pepper	pepper
1 medium-sized cauliflower	1 medium-sized cauliflower
1 red pepper	1 red pepper
2 stalks celery	2 stalks celery
2 tomatoes	2 tomatoes
30 ml/2 tbsp butter	2 tbsp butter
½ chicken stock cube	½ chicken stock cube
60 ml/4 tbsp water	4 tbsp water
125 g/¼ lb bean sprouts	⅔ cup bean sprouts
15 ml/1 tbsp soya sauce	1 tbsp soy sauce
45 ml/3 tbsp vegetable oil	3 tbsp vegetable oil
450 g/1 lb hot cooked rice (page 12)	6 cups hot cooked rice (page 12)

Sauce

	1¼ tbsp sugar
20 ml/1¼ tbsp sugar	2 tbsp white wine vinegar
30 ml/2 tbsp white wine vinegar	1 tbsp tomato paste
15 ml/1 tbsp tomato purée	1 tbsp soy sauce
15 ml/1 tbsp soya sauce	3 tbsp orange juice
45 ml/3 tbsp orange juice	1 tbsp cornstarch, mixed with 4 tbsp water
15 ml/1 tbsp cornflour, mixed with 60 ml/4 tbsp water	

To prepare: Break the eggs into a bowl and sprinkle with salt and pepper. Beat until they are well blended. Divide the cauliflower into very small flowerets. Remove the pith and seeds from the pepper and cut into small pieces. Cut the celery into 1.5 cm/½ in lengths. Cut the tomatoes into wedges. Combine all the sauce ingredients until they are well blended.

To cook: Put the butter, crumbled stock cube and water into a saucepan. When the butter has melted, add the cauliflower, celery, tomatoes, pepper, bean sprouts and soya sauce. Stir-fry for 1 minute. Reduce the heat to fairly low, cover the pan and simmer for 3–4 minutes. Remove from the heat and keep hot. Heat the oil in a medium-sized frying-pan. When the oil is hot, pour over the beaten eggs, tilting the pan so they spread out evenly. Cook without stirring for 1 minute. Remove from the heat and leave until the eggs are just about to set. Then gently stir a few times, being careful **not** to scramble. Remove from the heat and keep hot. Pour the sauce mixture into a small saucepan and bring to the boil, stirring until it thickens.

To serve: Arrange the cooked rice on a warmed platter. Top with the eggs and surround with the vegetable mixture. Pour the sauce over the top and take to the table.

set. Then gently stir a few times, being careful **not** to scramble. Remove the egg mixture from the pan and keep hot. Melt the butter in the pan and add the peas and tomatoes. Stir to blend. Sprinkle over the crumbled stock cube, water, soya sauce and sugar. Bring to the boil, then stir-fry for ½ minute.

To serve: Arrange the cooked rice on a warmed platter. Top with egg mixture and surround with pea and tomato mixture.

Cha shao quick-roast fish with leeks and tomatoes

METRIC/IMPERIAL	AMERICAN
2 slices root ginger	*2 slices root ginger*
Marinade (page 16)	*Marinade (page 16)*
1 kg/2 lb chunky fish, such as cod, haddock, carp, bream, pike, etc.	*2 lb chunky fish, such as cod, haddock, carp, bream, pike, etc.*
3 leeks	*3 leeks*
3 medium-sized tomatoes	*3 medium-sized tomatoes*
25 ml/1½ tbsp butter	*1½ tbsp butter*
½ chicken stock cube	*½ chicken stock cube*
5 ml/1 tsp sugar	*1 tsp sugar*
75–90 ml/5–6 tbsp water	*5–6 tbsp water*
15 ml/1 tbsp soya sauce	*1 tbsp soy sauce*
30 ml/2 tbsp dry sherry	*2 tbsp dry sherry*
450 g/1 lb hot cooked rice (page 12)	*6 cups hot cooked rice (page 12)*

To prepare: Peel and chop the ginger. Prepare the marinade. Cut the fish into 4–6 pieces. Sprinkle with the ginger, add to the marinade and baste well. Leave for 1 hour, basting occasionally. Clean the leeks thoroughly and cut into 1.5 cm/½ in lengths. Cut the tomatoes into quarters.

To cook: Arrange the fish pieces on a rack in a roasting pan. Put into the oven preheated to 230–240°C (450–475°F) Gas Mark 8–9. Roast for 10–12 minutes, turning once. Remove the fish from the oven and keep hot.

Put pan over moderate heat and add the butter. When the fat has melted, add the leeks and tomatoes. Stir and turn to coat well. Sprinkle with the crumbled stock cube, sugar, water, soya sauce and sherry. Increase the heat to fairly high, cover and cook for 2 minutes, adding more water if necessary.

To serve: Arrange the cooked rice on a warmed platter. Top with the fish and vegetables.

Fried rice with leftover meat and salad

The best leftovers for this dish are roast pork, roast lamb or roast chicken.

METRIC/IMPERIAL	AMERICAN
Fried rice (right)	*Fried rice (right)*
Chinese salad (right)	*Chinese salad (right)*
350–450 g/¾–1 lb cooked meat	*¾–1 lb cooked meat*
2 medium-sized onions	*2 medium-sized onions*
45 ml/3 tbsp vegetable oil	*3 tbsp vegetable oil*
15 ml/1 tbsp butter	*1 tbsp butter*
30 ml/2 tbsp soya sauce	*2 tbsp soy sauce*
15 ml/1 tbsp hoisin sauce	*1 tbsp hoisin sauce*
30 ml/2 tbsp dry sherry	*2 tbsp dry sherry*
7.5 ml/1½ tsp sugar	*1½ tsp sugar*
10 ml/2 tsp cornflour, mixed with 45 ml/3 tbsp cold chicken stock	*2 tsp cornstarch, mixed with 3 tbsp cold chicken stock*

To prepare: Prepare the fried rice and salad. Cut the meat into small, even-sized pieces. Slice the onions thinly.

To cook: Cook the fried rice and salad. Heat both the oil and butter in a frying-pan over moderate heat. When the fat has melted, add the onions. Stir and turn in the oil, then cook without stirring for 2 minutes. Add the meat, soya sauce, hoisin sauce, sherry and sugar. Increase the heat to fairly high

and stir-fry for 1½ minutes. Pour over the cornflour (cornstarch) mixture and stir until the sauce thickens.

To serve: Arrange the fried rice on a warmed platter. Top with the meat and salad mixture.

Fried rice with mixed vegetable salad

METRIC/IMPERIAL	AMERICAN
Fried Rice	**Fried Rice**
1 large onion	*1 large onion*
4 rashers streaky bacon	*4 slices fatty bacon*
4 eggs	*4 eggs*
60 ml/4 tbsp vegetable oil	*4 tbsp vegetable oil*
30 ml/2 tbsp butter	*2 tbsp butter*
125 g/¼ lb peas (shelled weight)	*½ cup peas (shelled weight)*
450 g/1 lb hot cooked rice (page 12)	*6 cups hot cooked rice (page 12)*
25 ml/1½ tbsp soya sauce	*1½ tbsp soy sauce*
Salad	**Salad**
1 firm cos lettuce	*1 firm romaine lettuce*
125 g/¼ lb bean sprouts	*⅔ cup bean sprouts*
2–3 tomatoes	*2–3 tomatoes*
2 stalks celery	*2 stalks celery*
½ bunch watercress	*½ bunch watercress*
1 clove garlic	*1 clove garlic*
2 slices root ginger	*2 slices root ginger*
2 spring onions	*2 scallions*
25 ml/1½ tbsp soya sauce	*1½ tbsp soy sauce*
30 ml/2 tbsp wine vinegar	*2 tbsp wine vinegar*
30 ml/2 tbsp clear broth (page 25)	*2 tbsp clear broth (page 25)*
7.5 ml/1½ tsp sugar	*1½ tsp sugar*
15 ml/1 tbsp sesame oil	*1 tbsp sesame oil*
15 ml/1 tbsp olive oil	*1 tbsp olive oil*

To prepare the fried rice: Slice the onion thinly. Cut the bacon, crosswise, into matchstick strips. Break the eggs into a bowl and beat until they are well blended.

To prepare the salad: Cut the vegetables into even-sized pieces. Crush the garlic and peel and grate the ginger. Cut the spring onions (scallions) into thin rounds. Combine the ginger, garlic, spring onions (scallions), soya sauce, vinegar, broth, sugar and oils until they are well blended.

To cook: For the rice, heat the oil and butter in a large saucepan over moderate heat. When the fat has melted, add the onion and bacon. Stir-fry for 1½ minutes. Pour the beaten eggs into one-half of the pan and add the peas to the other. Cook without stirring for 1 minute. Remove from the heat and leave until the eggs are just about to set. Stir the eggs into the other ingredients in the pan. Return the pan to the heat. Stir in the cooked rice and sprinkle with soya sauce. Keep hot. For the salad, put the vegetables into a bowl and pour over the liquid mixture. Toss well.

To serve: Arrange the fried rice on a warmed platter and spoon over the salad mixture.

Fried rice with mixed vegetable salad

Popular Chinese

Community cooking and eating have been the tradition and habit within the Chinese family since time immemorial. When one, or more, unexpected guest appears at the dining table, the meal can be quickly stretched by providing an extra stir-fried dish (which can be cooked within a few minutes), or some standby food, such as a red-cooked meat dish previously cooked and left cold, which can be heated up and served with confidence.

Three to four dishes served at a meal is considered quite limited fare in China, but they will be well balanced and embrace a good spread and variety of foods. Normally there will be a soup, which can easily be expanded to double the quantity by simply pouring in some extra broth and adding some thinly sliced vegetables, dried shrimps or mushrooms, for instance, to enhance the flavour. Then there will be one red-cooked dish (usually cooked in quantity for it can be reheated and used again), and to support these, there will be two to three stir-fried dishes, which can all be quickly cooked at the last moment. One of the stir-fried dishes could be a seafood dish such as shrimps, since if they are already shelled, they require no further cutting. They can also usually be cooked within a minute and the dish expanded if necessary to nearly double by adding some peas or chopped up vegetables (cucumber, celery, etc) and perhaps more broth and soya sauce. A meat stir-fried dish could also be served, with some broth enlivening the shredded meat, and flavoured with chopped pickles and quantities of fresh vegetables. Such a dish will be particularly flavoursome or even spicy, and it should go well with quantities of rice. For contrast, there could also be a dish of fish (whether dry fried, in sauce or in broth) or a dish of egg (steamed or stir-fried). All these last dishes are meant to be consumed at a single meal and only small quantities should therefore be prepared at a time.

When no great quantity of vegetables is represented in the soup, or in any of the other dishes, a separate dish of vegetables is often prepared and served to give the spread of food a better balance. If the vegetable is one of the soft ones (spinach, lettuce, tomato, mushrooms, peas, and bean sprouts) it is likely to be stir-fried, and served fresh and crisp. On the other hand, if the vegetable is hard or semi-hard (such as cauliflower, broccoli, aubergine, (eggplant), green beans, broad (fava or lima) beans, courgettes (zucchini) etc, it is likely to be braised with a small amount of broth, soya sauce and wine after an initial stir-frying, and the vegetables allowed to simmer under cover for a few minutes with a final stir-fry just before serving.

The selection of recipes in this section should give the reader ample choice to make up his or her menu for a typical three–four dish dinner. But when choosing be sure that at least one or two dishes are of the long-cooked variety, so that they can be 'retired' to cook long before the hour of the scheduled dinner, leaving you only the short-cooked, stir-fried dishes to attend to at the last moment; indeed, they can even be dealt with after the arrival of the guests.

dishes

北京広東四川

Chinese soup

Chinese soups are mostly drunk throughout the meal rather than served at the start of it. Although during banquets there may be several soups, served at intervals to punctuate the long series of courses, at a family dinner one soup will be placed on the table throughout the meal for 'lubricating', that is for drinking or sipping in between mouthfuls of solid foods. The majority of Chinese soups are clear soups, or consommés, into which a variety of ingredients (meats, seafoods, vegetables, fresh or dried) are added to create special and particular flavours. The number of distinctive soups which can be composed in this manner is almost unlimited, but all have as their base a good clear broth, as follows.

Clear broth

METRIC/IMPERIAL	AMERICAN
1 meaty chicken carcass	1 meaty chicken carcass
700 g/1½ lb pork spare ribs	1½ lb pork spare ribs
450 g/1 lb ham, bacon or beef bones	1 lb ham, bacon or beef bones
2 L/3½ pints water	2 quarts water
10 ml/2 tsp salt	2 tsp salt
10 ml/2 tsp dried shrimps (optional)	2 tsp dried shrimps (optional)

To prepare and cook: Put all the ingredients into a large, heavy-based saucepan. Bring to the boil and simmer gently for 1¾ hours, skimming any scum from the surface. Strain the broth and leave to cool. When it is cold, remove the fat from the surface and strain again.

This clear broth can be used as the basis for many Chinese soups, and is also often added in small quantities to other Chinese dishes.

Soup of the gods (egg-drop soup)

METRIC/IMPERIAL	AMERICAN
1 chicken stock cube	1 chicken stock cube
600 ml/1 pint hot clear broth (above)	2½ cups hot clear broth (above)
1 egg	1 egg
2–3 spring onions	2–3 scallions
5 ml/1 tsp sesame oil	1 tsp sesame oil
salt and pepper	salt and pepper

To prepare: Dissolve the stock cube in the broth. Break the egg into a bowl and beat until it is well blended. Cut the spring onions (scallions) into thin rounds.
To cook: Pour the broth into a saucepan and bring to the boil. Remove from the heat and drip the egg in a narrow stream along the prongs of a fork into the broth, trailing it over the surface. Do not stir until the egg has set (not more than 15 seconds).
To serve: Divide the spring onions (scallions) between individual serving bowls. Pour the broth and beaten egg into the bowls. Sprinkle with sesame oil and salt and pepper. This is one of the most popular soups in China, because it is economical and quick to make if you have the broth ready.

Clear broth

Spare rib and watercress soup

METRIC/IMPERIAL	AMERICAN
700 g/1 ½ lb pork spare ribs	1 ½ lb pork spare ribs
1 bunch watercress	1 bunch watercress
900 ml/1 ½ pints water	3 ¾ cups water
½ chicken stock cube	½ chicken stock cube
300 ml/½ pint clear broth (page 25)	1 ¼ cups clear broth (page 25)
salt and pepper	salt and pepper

To prepare: Cut the spare ribs into individual ribs, or chop into 4 cm/1½ in lengths. Clean the watercress thoroughly and trim.
To cook: Put the spare ribs into a heavy-based saucepan and pour in the water. Bring to the boil and simmer gently for 1½ hours, skimming any scum from the surface. Add the crumbled stock cube, broth and salt and pepper, and bring to the boil. Add the watercress and reboil.
To serve: Pour the soup into individual warmed bowls or a large tureen.

Beef, spinach and tomato soup

METRIC/IMPERIAL	AMERICAN
225 g/½ lb stewing beef	½ lb beef chuck
125–175 g/¼–⅓ lb spinach	1–1 ½ cups spinach
4–5 medium-sized tomatoes	4–5 medium-sized tomatoes
2 spring onions	2 scallions
2 slices root ginger (optional)	2 slices root ginger (optional)
600 ml/1 pint clear broth (page 25)	2 ½ cups clear broth (page 25)
½ chicken stock cube	½ chicken stock cube
salt and pepper	salt and pepper

To prepare: Cut the beef into 12–15 pieces. Clean the spinach thoroughly. Trim and chop. Cut the tomatoes into quarters and the spring onions (scallions) into 1.5 cm/½ in lengths. Peel and chop the ginger.
To cook: Put the beef into a large, heavy-based saucepan. Add the ginger and 600 ml/1 pint (2½ cups) of water. Bring to the boil and simmer gently for 1½ hours. Remove the ginger from the pan. Add the broth and crumbled stock cube and bring to the boil. Add the tomatoes, spinach, and spring onions (scallions) and return to the boil. Simmer gently for 3–4 minutes. Adjust the seasoning.
To serve: Pour the soup into individual warmed bowls or a large tureen.

Chicken mushroom soup

METRIC/IMPERIAL	AMERICAN
6 medium-sized Chinese dried mushrooms	6 medium-sized Chinese dried mushrooms
1 boned chicken breast, weighing about 125 g/¼ lb	1 boned chicken breast, weighing about ¼ lb
5 ml/1 tsp salt	1 tsp salt
15 ml/1 tbsp cornflour	1 tbsp cornstarch
½ egg white	½ egg white
225 g/½ lb mushrooms	1 ½ cups mushrooms
600 ml/1 pint clear broth (page 25)	2 ½ cups clear broth (page 25)
15 ml/1 tbsp soya sauce	1 tbsp soy sauce
salt and pepper	salt and pepper

Beef, spinach and tomato soup

To prepare: Soak the dried mushrooms in 300 ml/½ pint (1¼ cups) of water for 30 minutes. Remove the stalks and cut the caps into quarters. Put the caps and soaking water into a small saucepan and bring to the boil. Simmer gently for 15 minutes. Cut the chicken meat into thin strips. Rub all over with salt and cornflour (cornstarch) and coat with egg white. Remove the stalks from the fresh mushrooms, and cut them into thin slices.

To cook: Pour the broth into a large saucepan. Add the dried mushrooms and soaking liquid, and fresh mushrooms. Bring to the boil and simmer gently for 5–6 minutes. Add the chicken strips and simmer for 5–6 minutes. Add the soya sauce and adjust the seasoning.

To serve: Pour the soup into individual warmed bowls or a large tureen.

Hot and sour soup

METRIC/IMPERIAL	AMERICAN
6–8 medium-sized Chinese dried mushrooms	6–8 medium-sized Chinese dried mushrooms
1 cake bean curd	1 cake bean curd
1 egg	1 egg
45–60 ml/3–4 tbsp wine vinegar	3–4 tbsp wine vinegar
2.5 ml/½ tsp black pepper	½ tsp black pepper
30 ml/2 tbsp cornflour	2 tbsp cornstarch
90 ml/6 tbsp water	6 tbsp water
900 ml/1½ pints clear broth (page 25)	3¾ cups clear broth (page 25)
1 chicken stock cube	1 chicken stock cube
30 ml/2 tbsp soya sauce	2 tbsp soy sauce
60 ml/4 tbsp shrimps (shelled weight)	4 tbsp shrimps (shelled weight)

To prepare: Soak the dried mushrooms in 300 ml/½ pint (1¼ cups) of water for 30 minutes. Remove the stalks and cut the caps into quarters. Reserve the soaking water. Cut the bean curd into small cubes. Break the egg into a bowl and beat until well blended. Combine the vinegar, pepper, cornflour (cornstarch) and water until they are well blended.

To cook: Put the dried mushrooms and soaking water into a saucepan. Add the broth, crumbled stock cube, soya sauce, bean curd and shrimps. Bring to the boil over gentle heat. Drip the egg in a narrow stream along the prongs of a fork into the broth mixture, trailing it over the surface. Do not stir until the egg has set (not more than 15 seconds). Pour in the vinegar mixture and stir. Heat gently for 1 minute.

To serve: Pour the soup into individual warmed bowls or a large tureen.

Shrimp, chicken and sweetcorn soup

METRIC/IMPERIAL	AMERICAN
1 boned chicken breast, weighing about 125 g/¼ lb	1 boned chicken breast, weighing about ¼ lb
300 ml/½ pint cold clear broth (page 25)	1¼ cups cold clear broth (page 25)
25 ml/1½ tbsp cornflour	1½ tbsp cornstarch
425 g/14 oz tin sweetcorn	14 oz can sweetcorn
125–175 g/¼–⅓ lb shrimps (shelled weight)	¼–⅓ lb shrimps (shelled weight)
125 g/¼ lb peas (shelled weight)	½ cup peas (shelled weight)
1 chicken stock cube	1 chicken stock cube
salt and pepper	salt and pepper

To prepare: Dice the chicken into cubes. Combine the broth with the cornflour (cornstarch) until they are well blended.

To cook: Put the sweetcorn into a large saucepan. Add the shrimps, chicken, peas, crumbled stock cube and 300 ml/½ pint (1¼ cups) of water. Bring to the boil and simmer gently for 2–3 minutes. Add the broth mixture, and stir well. Adjust the seasoning. Heat for 1 minute more, stirring constantly.

To serve: Pour the soup into individual warmed bowls or a large tureen.

Mixed vegetable soup with shredded bacon

METRIC/IMPERIAL	AMERICAN
75 g/3 oz transparent pea-starch noodles (optional)	3 oz transparent pea-starch noodles (optional)
2 rashers streaky bacon	2 slices fatty bacon
75 g/3 oz French beans	½ cup green beans
½ red pepper	½ red pepper
1 medium-sized onion	1 medium-sized onion
2 stalks celery	2 stalks celery
3 medium-sized tomatoes	3 medium-sized tomatoes
3–4 lettuce leaves	3–4 lettuce leaves
50 g/2 oz watercress	½ cup watercress
2 spring onions	2 scallions
1¼ L/2 pints clear broth (page 25)	5 cups clear broth (page 25)
1 chicken stock cube	1 chicken stock cube
25 ml/1½ tbsp soya sauce	1½ tbsp soy sauce
salt and pepper	salt and pepper

To prepare: Soak the noodles in warm water for 10 minutes, then drain. Cut the bacon, crosswise, into matchstick strips. Trim the beans and cut in half. Remove the pith and seeds from the pepper, then cut into thin slices. Slice the onion thinly. Cut the celery diagonally into 2.5 cm/1 in lengths, then cut the tomatoes into wedges. Clean the lettuce and watercress thoroughly and chop. Cut the spring onions (scallions) into 1.5 cm/½ in lengths.

To cook: Pour the broth into a large saucepan. Add the bacon, beans, celery, onion, pepper and crumbled stock cube. Bring to the boil and simmer gently for 15 minutes. Add the tomatoes, watercress, lettuce, soya sauce and spring onions (scallions). Simmer for 5 minutes. Adjust the seasoning.

To serve: Pour the soup into individual warmed bowls or a large tureen.

Ingredients for a mixed vegetable soup

Watermelon soup

METRIC/IMPERIAL
4–5 Chinese dried mushrooms
1 large piece bamboo shoot
50 g/2 oz cooked ham
2 slices root ginger
1 medium-sized watermelon
600 ml/1 pint stock
1 chicken stock cube
10 ml/2 tsp dried shrimps
30 ml/2 tbsp dry sherry
2.5 ml/½ tsp salt

AMERICAN
4–5 Chinese dried mushrooms
1 large piece bamboo shoot
2 oz cooked ham
2 slices root ginger
1 medium-sized watermelon
2 ½ cups stock
1 chicken stock cube
2 tsp dried shrimps
2 tbsp dry sherry
½ tsp salt

To prepare: Soak the dried mushrooms in 300 ml/½ pint of water for 30 minutes. Remove the stalks and cut the caps into quarters. Cut the bamboo shoot into thin slices and cut the ham into small dice. Peel and shred the ginger. Halve the melon crosswise and scoop out the pulp and seeds from the lower half. Slice about a quarter of the flesh to the same size as the bamboo shoots. Scoop out some of the seeds and pulp from the upper half of the melon and use the latter as a 'lid' for the lower half. (Reduce the height if necessary.)

To cook: Heat the stock in a saucepan. Add all the ingredients, except the melon shells, and bring to the boil gently. Simmer for 30 minutes. Stand the scooped-out melon half in a heatproof bowl and pour in the contents of the pan. Close the top with the 'lid'. Put the bowl in a steamer and steam for 45 minutes (or improvise by placing the bowl in a large saucepan with about a 2.5 cm./1 in layer of boiling water, and boil for 5–6 minutes).

To serve: Remove the bowl from the steamer and ladle out the soup from the melon. Serves four.

Watermelon soup

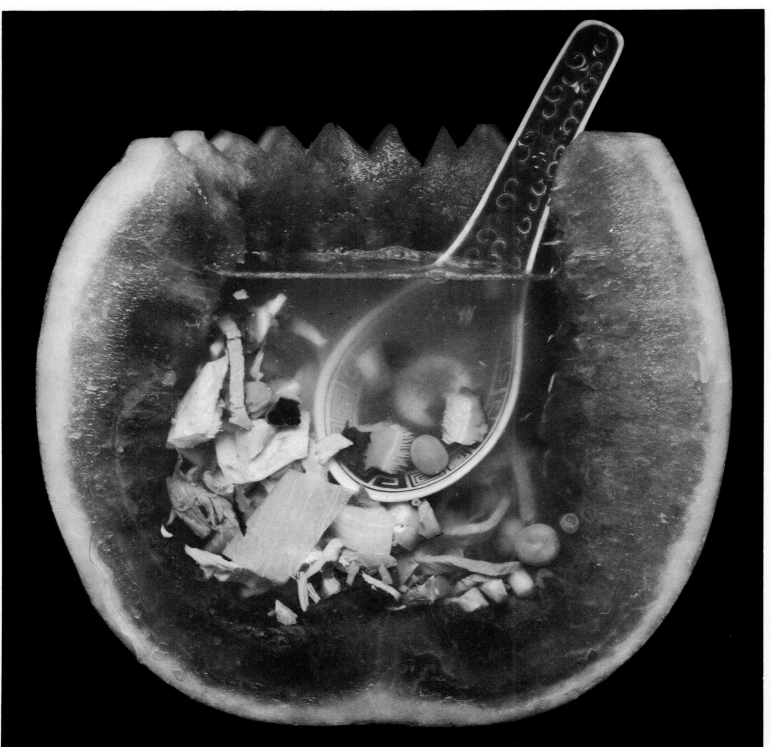

Noodle Dishes

Next to rice, noodles rank as the most important and popular bulk food in China. The dishes made from noodles differ from western spaghetti and macaroni dishes in that a greater range of vegetables and other ingredients are incorporated into the cooking and presentation, and cheese and other dairy products are not added. Chinese noodle dishes are often double-decker affairs, where the noodles, which have been tossed in flavoured oil, or served in a sauce or in a bowl of soup, are topped with a substantial garnish. Thus a noodle dish can be, and often is, a meal in itself.

Noodles in sauce (birthday long-life noodles)

METRIC/IMPERIAL	AMERICAN
1–1½ kg/2–3 lb knuckle of pork	2–3 lb knuckle of pork
55 ml/3½ tbsp soya sauce	3½ tbsp soy sauce
45 ml/3 tbsp dry sherry	3 tbsp dry sherry
725 ml/1¼ pints clear broth (page 25)	3 cups clear broth (page 25)
450 g/1 lb Chinese noodles	1 lb Chinese noodles
3–4 eggs	3–4 eggs
soya sauce (for browning the eggs – it can be re-used afterwards)	soy sauce (for browning the eggs – it can be re-used afterwards)

To prepare and cook: Put the knuckle into a flameproof casserole. Cover with water and bring to the boil. Simmer gently for 40 minutes, skimming any scum from the surface. Add the soya sauce and sherry. Reduce the heat to very low, place an asbestos sheet under the pan, or cook in the oven preheated to 150°C (300°F) Gas Mark 2 for 1 hour. Add the broth and simmer gently for a further 1 hour. Scrape the meat off the knuckle bones. Cook the noodles in boiling, salted water for 7–8 minutes and drain. Add to the sauce produced by cooking the broth with the knuckle. Hard-boil the eggs, shell and simmer in a shallow panful of soya sauce (enough to cover the bottom of the pan to a 1.5 cm/½ in layer), turning them over about 5–6 times for 15 minutes, until they are brown.

To serve: Either divide the noodle mixture between individual bowls or put into one large bowl. Decorate the top of the noodles — which should be half submerged in the sauce — with the eggs and meat from the knuckle. In China the knuckle is often served whole, or cut into 2–3 pieces, then served on top of the noodles with the eggs. These noodles are traditionally served at birthday celebrations, hence the name 'long life'.

Prawns or shrimps and chicken-wing soup noodles

METRIC/IMPERIAL	AMERICAN
350 g/¾ lb Chinese noodles or spaghetti	¾ lb Chinese noodles or spaghetti
175–225 g/⅓–½ lb spinach or cabbage heart	1½–2 cups spinach or cabbage heart
3 cloves garlic	3 cloves garlic
6 chicken wings	6 chicken wings
45 ml/3 tbsp vegetable oil	3 tbsp vegetable oil
45 ml/3 tbsp soya sauce	3 tbsp soy sauce
75 ml/5 tbsp water	5 tbsp water
1¼ L/2 pints clear broth (page 25)	5 cups clear broth (page 25)
5 ml/1 tsp sugar	1 tsp sugar
45 ml/3 tbsp dry sherry	3 tbsp dry sherry
1 chicken stock cube	1 chicken stock cube
30 ml/2 tbsp butter	2 tbsp butter
225 g/½ lb prawns (shelled weight)	½ lb shrimps (shelled weight)

To prepare: Cook the noodles in boiling, salted water for 7–8 minutes (spaghetti for 12 minutes), and drain. Rinse in cold water to keep separate. Clean the spinach or cabbage heart thoroughly. Trim and chop. Crush the garlic. Chop the chicken wings at the joints.

To cook: Heat the oil in a small saucepan. Add the chicken wings and stir-fry for 3–4 minutes. Add the soya sauce, water and 75 ml/5 tbsp of broth. Bring to the boil and simmer gently for 30 minutes, turning the wings two or three times. Add the sugar and sherry. Simmer gently for a further 20 minutes, stirring occasionally. Pour the remaining broth into a large saucepan. Add the crumbled stock cube, noodles and spinach. Bring to the boil and simmer gently for 5 minutes. Put the butter and garlic into a small frying-pan. Stir-fry for a few seconds. Add the prawns or shrimps and stir-fry for ½ minute. Simmer gently for 1½ minutes.

To serve: Pour the broth and noodles into individual warmed bowls and top with spinach, chicken and prawns (shrimps).

Shredded chicken and ham soup noodles

METRIC/IMPERIAL	AMERICAN
350 g/¾ lb Chinese noodles or spaghetti	¾ lb Chinese noodles or spaghetti
125 g/¼ lb ham	⅔ cup ham
125 g/¼ lb roasted chicken meat	⅔ cup roasted chicken meat
175–225 g/⅓–½ lb spinach	1½–2 cups spinach
1 chicken stock cube	1 chicken stock cube
900 ml/1½ pints clear broth (page 25)	3¾ cups clear broth (page 25)
30 ml/2 tbsp vegetable oil	2 tbsp vegetable oil
15 ml/1 tbsp butter	1 tbsp butter
15 ml/1 tbsp soya sauce	1 tbsp soy sauce

To prepare: Cook the noodles in boiling, salted water for 7–8 minutes (spaghetti for 12 minutes) and drain. Rinse in cold water to keep separate. Cut the ham and chicken meat into matchstick shreds. Clean the spinach thoroughly. Trim and chop.

To cook: Add the crumbled stock cube to the broth and bring to the boil. Add the noodles or spaghetti and simmer gently for 2 minutes. Heat the oil and butter in a frying-pan over high heat. When the fat has melted, add the spinach. Stir and turn for 1 minute. Sprinkle with soya sauce and stir-fry for 1 minute.

To serve: Pour the noodles and soup into a large tureen, or individual warmed bowls, and top with shredded ham, chicken and spinach. When spinach is not in season, green cabbage heart can be used instead but this will require an extra 3 minutes frying time, with 30–45 ml/2–3 tbsp of clear broth sprinkled over it.

Chow Mein

Chow meins are fried noodles. Here the noodles which have been boiled and drained are fried first in a flavoured oil, then topped with a variety of ingredients, such as meat, vegetables and seafood.

Chow mein with seafood

METRIC/IMPERIAL	AMERICAN
350 g/¾ lb Chinese noodles or spaghetti	¾ lb Chinese noodles or spaghetti
1 medium-sized onion	1 medium-sized onion
2 rashers bacon	2 slices bacon
55 ml/3 ½ tbsp vegetable oil	3 ½ tbsp vegetable oil
225 g/½ lb tin clams or crabmeat	½ lb can clams or crabmeat
45 ml/3 tbsp soya sauce	3 tbsp soy sauce

Garnish	**Garnish**
3 slices root ginger	3 slices root ginger
3 cloves garlic	3 cloves garlic
3 spring onions	3 scallions
½ red pepper	½ red pepper
40 ml/2 ½ tbsp butter	2 ½ tbsp butter
6 oysters	6 oysters
225 g/½ lb prawns or mussels (shelled weight)	½ lb shrimps or mussels (shelled weight)
salt and pepper	salt and pepper
5 ml/1 tsp sugar	1 tsp sugar
30 ml/2 tbsp dry sherry	2 tbsp dry sherry

To prepare: Cook the noodles in boiling, salted water for 7–8 minutes (spaghetti for 12 minutes), and drain. Rinse in cold water to keep separate. Shred the onion, bacon and ginger. Crush the garlic. Cut the spring onions (scallions) into 2.5 cm/1 in lengths. Remove the pith and seeds from the pepper and shred.

To cook: Heat the oil in a large frying-pan over high heat. Add the onion and bacon and stir-fry for ½ minute. Cook for 1 minute. Add the clams or crabmeat and 30 ml/2 tbsp of the soya sauce. Stir and turn in the fat for 1 minute. Pour in the noodles or spaghetti and sprinkle with the remaining soya sauce. Stir-fry for 1 minute. Reduce the heat to low and simmer gently for 3–4 minutes, until they have heated through. Meanwhile, heat the butter in a small frying-pan over high heat. When the fat has melted, add the ginger, garlic, pepper, oysters and prawns (shrimps). Stir-fry for 1 minute. Sprinkle with spring onions (scallions), salt and pepper, sugar and sherry. Stir-fry for 1 minute.

To serve: Spoon the noodles, clams, etc from the large pan into a large, warmed bowl. Spoon over the contents of the smaller pan as a garnish.

Chow mein with seafood

Chicken and bacon chow mein with bean sprouts, mushrooms and spring onions (scallions)

METRIC/IMPERIAL	AMERICAN
350 g/¾ lb Chinese noodles or spaghetti	¾ lb Chinese noodles or spaghetti
1 medium-sized onion	1 medium-sized onion
3 rashers streaky bacon	3 slices fatty bacon
6–8 medium-sized Chinese dried mushrooms	6–8 medium-sized Chinese dried mushrooms
6–8 large button mushrooms	6–8 large button mushrooms
3 spring onions	3 scallions
½ chicken stock cube	½ chicken stock cube
60 ml/4 tbsp hot clear broth (page 25)	4 tbsp hot clear broth (page 25)
1 boned chicken breast, weighing about 175 g/⅓ lb	1 boned chicken breast, weighing about ⅓ lb
55 ml/3½ tbsp vegetable oil	3½ tbsp vegetable oil
40 ml/2½ tbsp soya sauce	2½ tbsp soy sauce
40 ml/2½ tbsp butter	2½ tbsp butter
125 g/¼ lb bean sprouts	⅔ cup bean sprouts
25 ml/1½ tbsp dry sherry	1½ tbsp dry sherry

To prepare: Cook the noodles in boiling, salted water for 7–8 minutes (spaghetti for 12 minutes), and drain. Rinse in cold water to keep separate. Shred the onion and bacon. Soak the dried mushrooms in 300 ml/½ pint (1¼ cups) of water for 30 minutes. Remove the stalks and shred the caps. Remove the stalks from the fresh mushrooms and shred the caps. Cut the spring onions (scallions) into 2.5 cm/1 in lengths. Dissolve the stock cube in the broth. Shred the chicken.

To cook: Heat the oil in a large frying-pan over moderate heat. Add the bacon, onion and dried mushrooms. Stir-fry for ½ minute, then cook for 1½ minutes. Stir-fry again for ½ minute. Add the cooked noodles. Turn them thoroughly in the flavoured fat. Reduce the heat to low, sprinkle with half the soya sauce and half the broth, and stir and turn the noodles again a few times. Cook for 2 minutes. Meanwhile, heat the butter in a small frying-pan. When the fat has melted, add the chicken, fresh mushrooms, bean sprouts and spring onions (scallions). Stir-fry for 2 minutes. Sprinkle with the remaining soya sauce, broth and the sherry. Stir-fry for ½ minute.

To serve: Pour the noodles, dried mushrooms and bacon into a large, warmed serving bowl. Top with the chicken, mushrooms and spring onions (scallions).

Cha chiang mein (or Peking hot-tossed noodles)

METRIC/IMPERIAL	AMERICAN
450 g/1 lb Chinese noodles or spaghetti	1 lb Chinese noodles or spaghetti
1 medium-sized onion	1 medium-sized onion
4 cloves garlic	4 cloves garlic
45 ml/3 tbsp vegetable oil	3 tbsp vegetable oil
25 ml/1½ tbsp lard or butter	1½ tbsp lard or butter
350 g/¾ lb minced pork	¾ lb ground pork
5 ml/1 tsp sugar	1 tsp sugar
25 ml/1½ tbsp soya sauce	1½ tbsp soy sauce
15 ml/1 tbsp soya paste or hoisin sauce	1 tbsp soy paste or hoisin sauce
30 ml/2 tbsp dry sherry	2 tbsp dry sherry
30 ml/2 tbsp water	2 tbsp water

Garnish

225 g/½ lb bean sprouts	1⅓ cups bean sprouts
⅓ medium-sized cucumber	⅓ medium-sized cucumber
6 medium-sized radishes	6 medium-sized radishes
2 medium-sized gherkins	2 medium-sized gherkins
4 spring onions	4 scallions

To prepare: Cook the noodles in boiling, salted water for 7–8 minutes (spaghetti for 12 minutes). Do not prepare or drain until just before serving. Chop the onion and crush the garlic. Wash the bean sprouts and drain thoroughly. Cut the cucumber into long matchstick shreds. Cut the radishes and gherkins into similar shreds, and the spring onions (scallions) into 4 cm/1½ in lengths.

To cook: Heat the oil and fat in a saucepan over high heat. Add the onion and stir-fry for ½ minute. Add the pork and garlic and stir-fry for 3 minutes. Add the sugar, soya sauce and soya paste. Stir and simmer gently. Add the sherry and water. Reduce the heat to low and simmer for 5–6 minutes.

To serve: Drain the hot noodles and pour them into a large, warmed serving bowl. Pour the meat and sauce into the centre of the noodles. Surround with bowls of bean sprouts, cucumber, gherkins, radishes and spring onions (scallions). The diners should transfer a proportion of the meat sauce and noodles to individual bowls and top with a selection of the shredded vegetable garnish. A few drops of Chinese aromatic vinegar (if available, otherwise use wine vinegar and sesame oil) are sometimes sprinkled over the contents of the bowl. This is a very popular dish from Peking.

Pork Dishes

Pork can be cooked in several different ways: red-cooked, quick-roasted or marinated, quick-fried diced cubes in soya paste, quick-fried sliced or shredded with vegetables. Minced (ground) pork is generally made into meatballs, the best known dish of which is 'Lion's Head' meatballs, a traditional banquet dish (page 40).

Red-cooked pork with chestnuts (below)
Red-cooked pork with spring onions (scallions) and eggs (right)

Basic red-cooked pork

METRIC/IMPERIAL	AMERICAN
1½–2 kg/3–4 lb belly of pork	3–4 lb belly of pork
7.5 ml/1½ tsp sugar	1½ tsp sugar
125 ml/4 fl oz water	½ cup water
70 ml/4½ tbsp soya sauce	4½ tbsp soy sauce
75 ml/5 tbsp dry sherry	5 tbsp dry sherry

To prepare: Cut the pork through the skin, lean and fat, into 4 cm/1½ in pieces. Combine the sugar, water and soya sauce until they are well blended.
To cook: Put the pork pieces into a flameproof casserole. Pour over enough boiling water to cover. Cook for 15 minutes, then

drain off all the water. Pour in the soya sauce mixture. Stir and turn the pork pieces in the sauce until they are well coated. Put the casserole into the oven preheated to 150°C (300°F) Gas Mark 2. Cook for 1 hour, stirring twice. Stir in the sherry. Re-cover the casserole and return to the oven to cook for a further 1 hour, stirring twice.

To serve: Serve straight from the casserole. This is an excellent accompaniment to rice, and also re-heats very well. Serves four to six people.

Red-cooked pork with chestnuts

Repeat the recipe for Basic red-cooked pork (page 36). Cook 225 g/½ lb (1⅓ cups) of peeled chestnuts in boiling water for 30 minutes. Drain, then add to the pork with an extra 15 ml/1 tbsp of soya sauce during the final hour's cooking period. Serves four to six people.

Red-cooked pork with spring onions (scallions) and eggs

Repeat the recipe for Basic red-cooked pork (page 36). Clean and cut about 4–5 spring onions (scallions) into 2.5 cm/1 in pieces. Stir-fry in 55 ml/3½ tbsp of vegetable oil for 3 minutes, with 3 cloves of crushed garlic. Simmer 4 hard-boiled eggs in 150 ml/¼ pint (⅝ cup) of soya sauce for 7–8 minutes, or until brown. Use spring onions (scallions) as a base for pork and surround the pork with the eggs. This dish is also known as the 'Pork of Four Happiness'. Serves four to six people.

Cha shao quick-roast pork

METRIC/IMPERIAL	AMERICAN
1 kg/2¼ lb fillet of pork, in one piece	2¼ lb tenderloin of pork, in one piece

Marinade | **Marinade**

METRIC/IMPERIAL	AMERICAN
45 ml/3 tbsp soya sauce	3 tbsp soy sauce
15 ml/1 tbsp soya paste	1 tbsp soy paste
15 ml/1 tbsp hoisin sauce (optional)	1 tbsp hoisin sauce (optional)
30 ml/2 tbsp dry sherry	2 tbsp dry sherry
10 ml/2 tsp sugar	2 tsp sugar
15 ml/1 tbsp tomato purée	1 tbsp tomato paste
15 ml/1 tbsp vegetable oil	1 tbsp vegetable oil

To prepare: Combine all the marinade ingredients until they are well blended. Add the pork and baste well. Leave for 1½ hours, stirring the pork every 30 minutes.

To cook: Arrange the pork piece on a rack in a roasting pan. Put into the oven preheated to 230–240°C (450–475°F) Gas Mark 8–9. Roast for 12–15 minutes, turning twice.

To serve: Cut the pork across the grain into thin slices. Because of the action of the heat and marinade, the edge of the pork is a very different colour from the middle, which should be just freshly cooked. The dripping can be made into a gravy by adding 60–75 ml/4–5 tbsp of clear broth (page 25) and 15 ml/1 tbsp of soya sauce, then stirring them together over moderate heat for ½ minute. Any leftover pork can be served cold. Serves four to six.

Barbecued spare ribs

METRIC/IMPERIAL	AMERICAN
1½ kg/3 lb pork spare ribs	3 lb pork spare ribs
3–4 slices root ginger	3–4 slices root ginger
2 medium-sized onions	2 medium-sized onions
45 ml/3 tbsp vegetable oil	3 tbsp vegetable oil
75 ml/5 tbsp soya sauce	5 tbsp soy sauce
75 ml/5 tbsp water	5 tbsp water
30 ml/2 tbsp hoisin sauce	2 tbsp hoisin sauce
5 ml/1 tsp sugar	1 tsp sugar
75 ml/5 tbsp dry sherry	5 tbsp dry sherry
salt and pepper	salt and pepper
75 ml/5 tbsp clear broth (page 25)	5 tbsp clear broth (page 25)

To prepare: Cut the spare ribs into individual ribs. Blanch them in boiling water for 2 minutes, then drain. Peel and shred the ginger. Slice the onions thinly.

To cook: Put the ribs and oil into a flameproof casserole. Bring to the boil and stir-fry for 5 minutes. Add the soya sauce, water, hoisin sauce, sugar, ginger and onions. Stir and turn until the ingredients are well blended. Put the casserole into the oven preheated to 150°C (300°F) Gas Mark 2. Cook for 1 hour, stirring twice. At the first stirring, add the sherry and adjust the seasoning. Remove the ribs and place them side by side on the bottom of a roasting pan. Put them into the oven and increase the temperature to 230°C (450°F) Gas Mark 8. Roast for 12–15 minutes. Set the casserole over moderate heat. Add the broth and stir-fry for 2–3 minutes.

To serve: Arrange the ribs on a warmed dish. The gravy can be poured over before serving. Serves four to six.

Quick-fried pork in Peking sauce

METRIC/IMPERIAL	AMERICAN
700 g/1½ lb leg of pork	1½ lb leg of pork
15 ml/1 tbsp cornflour	1 tbsp cornstarch
60 ml/4 tbsp vegetable oil	4 tbsp vegetable oil
25 ml/1½ tbsp lard	1½ tbsp lard

Sauce | **Sauce**

METRIC/IMPERIAL	AMERICAN
30 ml/2 tbsp soya paste	2 tbsp soy paste
15 ml/1 tbsp hoisin sauce	1 tbsp hoisin sauce
25 ml/1½ tbsp soya sauce	1½ tbsp soy sauce
7.5 ml/1½ tsp sugar	1½ tsp sugar
10 ml/2 tsp cornflour	2 tsp cornstarch
25 ml/1½ tbsp dry sherry	1½ tbsp dry sherry

To prepare: Cut the pork into 1.5 cm/½ in cubes. Rub all over with cornflour (cornstarch) and a quarter of the oil. Combine all the sauce ingredients until they are well blended.

To cook: Heat the remaining oil in a large frying-pan over high heat. When the oil is very hot, add the pork cubes. Stir-fry for 2½ minutes. Push them to one side of the pan. Add the lard to the pan and reduce the heat to moderate. When the fat has melted, add the sauce mixture and stir and turn in the pan until the sauce and fat are well blended. Stir the pork cubes into the thickening sauce. Stir and turn them in the sauce a few times.

To serve: Turn into a warmed dish.

Quick-fried pork with peppers

METRIC/IMPERIAL	AMERICAN
450 g/1 lb leg of pork	1 lb leg of pork
5 ml/1 tsp salt	1 tsp salt
25 ml/1½ tbsp cornflour	1½ tbsp cornstarch
75 ml/5 tbsp vegetable oil	5 tbsp vegetable oil
1 medium-sized green pepper	1 medium-sized green pepper
1 medium-sized red pepper	1 medium-sized red pepper
25 ml/1½ tbsp lard	1½ tbsp lard
25 ml/1½ tbsp soya sauce	1½ tbsp soy sauce
15 ml/1 tbsp hoisin sauce	1 tbsp hoisin sauce
2.5 ml/½ tsp sugar	½ tsp sugar
30 ml/2 tbsp dry sherry	2 tbsp dry sherry

To prepare: Cut the pork into thin slices. Rub all over with the salt, cornflour (cornstarch) and 15 ml/1 tbsp of the oil. Remove the pith and seeds from the peppers and cut them into approximately same-sized pieces as the pork.

To cook: Heat the remaining oil in a large frying-pan over high heat. When the oil is very hot, add the pork slices and stir-fry for 2 minutes. Push them to one side of the pan. Add the lard to the other side of the pan. When the fat has melted, add the peppers. Stir and turn them in the hot fat for 1 minute. Stir the pork into the peppers. Sprinkle with soya sauce, hoisin sauce, sugar and sherry. Stir-fry for 1 minute.

To serve: Turn into a warmed dish.

Barbecued spare ribs

Lion's head meatballs

METRIC/IMPERIAL	AMERICAN
225 g/½ lb belly of pork	½ lb belly of pork
1 medium-sized onion	1 medium-sized onion
2 cloves garlic	2 cloves garlic
4 medium-sized water chestnuts	4 medium-sized water chestnuts
450 g/1 lb minced pork	1 lb ground pork
60 ml/4 tbsp soya sauce	4 tbsp soy sauce
5 ml/1 tsp salt	1 tsp salt
25 ml/1½ tbsp water	1½ tbsp water
15 ml/1 tbsp cornflour	1 tbsp cornstarch
125 g/¼ lb transparent pea-starch noodles	¼ lb transparent pea-starch noodles
40 ml/2½ tbsp vegetable oil	2½ tbsp vegetable oil
150 ml/¼ pint clear broth (page 25)	⅝ cup clear broth (page 25)
30 ml/2 tbsp dry sherry	2 tbsp dry sherry

To prepare: Shred or chop the belly of pork. Slice the onion thinly. Shred the garlic. Cut the water chestnuts and chop finely. Mix the minced (ground) pork with the chopped belly of pork, the onion, garlic, water chestnuts, half the soya sauce, the salt, water and cornflour (cornstarch). Beat until they are well blended. Soak the noodles in hot water. Form the pork mixture into four equal-sized balls.

To cook: Put the oil into a flameproof casserole. Add the meatballs and stir and turn them in the oil. Cook over low heat for 7–8 minutes, until the meatballs are golden. Cover the casserole and put into the oven preheated to 150°C (300°F) Gas Mark 2. Cook for 2 hours, stirring gently every 30 minutes. Remove the meatballs from the casserole and keep hot. Add the broth, sherry and remaining soya sauce to the casserole. Stir a few times. When the mixture boils, add the noodles. Cook gently for 8–10 minutes (by this time, the noodles should have absorbed most or all of the liquid).

To serve: Turn half the noodles into a warmed bowl, and spread out evenly. Arrange three meatballs in the middle of the 'bed', and place the last meatball at the centre, on top of the others. Use the remaining noodles to drape the 'lion's head' in the form of a mane. This is a famous banquet dish in China. The long cooking and the pork fat will make the meatballs succulent, yet the water chestnuts keep the texture crunchy.

Stir-fried pork with mushrooms

METRIC/IMPERIAL	AMERICAN
½ kg/1 lb lean pork	1 lb lean pork
30 ml/2 tbsp soya sauce	2 tbsp soy sauce
25 ml/1½ tbsp hoisin sauce	1½ tbsp hoisin sauce
55 ml/3½ tbsp vegetable oil	3½ tbsp vegetable oil
15 ml/1 tbsp sherry	1 tbsp sherry
5 ml/1 tsp sugar	1 tsp sugar
25 ml/1½ tbsp tomato purée	1½ tbsp tomato paste
5 ml/1 tsp chilli sauce	1 tsp chilli sauce
6–8 medium mushrooms	6–8 medium mushrooms
25 ml/1½ tbsp butter	1½ tbsp butter
7.5 ml/1½ tsp cornflour, blended with 45 ml/3 tbsp water	1½ tsp cornstarch, blended with 3 tbsp water

To prepare: Cut the pork into approximately 4 cm/1½ in by 2.5 cm/1 in slices. Rub with half the soya sauce, hoisin sauce, vegetable oil, sherry, sugar, tomato purée (paste) and chilli sauce. Leave for 30 minutes. Remove the stalks from the mushrooms and cut both the stalks and caps into quarters.

To cook: Heat the butter in a small saucepan. Add the mushroom stalks and stir-fry for 2 minutes. Add the mushroom caps and stir-fry for 1 minute. Heat the remaining oil in a large frying-pan over high heat. Add the pork and marinade and stir-fry for 2 minutes. Add the mushrooms from the saucepan and the remaining soya sauce, hoisin sauce, sugar, tomato purée (paste), sherry and chilli sauce. Stir-fry for 1½ minutes. Pour over the cornflour (cornstarch) mixture and stir until the sauce thickens.

To serve: Turn into a warmed dish.

Stir-fried pork with mushrooms (above) Lion's head meatballs (right)

Chicken Dishes

To the Chinese, chicken and pork share one quality: a 'neutral savouriness', which enables them to combine easily and successfully with a great many other ingredients. Hence there are more chicken and pork dishes than there are of any other poultry or meat. On the whole, chicken is cooked in the same manner as pork, except when it is stir-fried, although the cooking time required is much shorter. Chicken is used more often in soups and 'semi-soup' dishes, where the addition of vegetables and liquid greatly increase the volume and weight of the other ingredients — thus making for greater economy. Such dishes are often served in conjunction with the drier or spicier stir-fried dishes, and with rice.

Slow-simmered chicken

METRIC/IMPERIAL	AMERICAN
1 × 1½–2 kg/3–4 lb chicken	1 × 3–4 lb chicken
2 medium-sized onions	2 medium-sized onions
1 medium-sized Chinese or Savoy cabbage	1 medium-sized Chinese or Savoy cabbage
3–4 slices root ginger	3–4 slices root ginger
10 ml/2 tsp salt	2 tsp salt
1 chicken stock cube	1 chicken stock cube
45 ml/3 tbsp Chinese snow pickles, or gherkins	3 tbsp Chinese snow pickles, or gherkins

To prepare: Blanch the chicken in boiling water for 6 minutes, skimming any scum from the surface. Drain well. Cut the onions into quarters. Cut the cabbage into quarters, then the quarters into halves. Peel and chop the ginger. Rub the chicken, inside and out, with the salt and stuff with a mixture of ginger, crumbled stock cube, onions and pickles.
To cook: Put the stuffed chicken in a flameproof casserole with 1¼ L/2 pints (5 cups) of water. Bring to the boil. Put the casserole into the oven preheated to 180°C (350°F) Gas Mark 4. Cook for 1⅓ hours, turning the chicken once. Put the cabbage underneath the chicken and return the casserole to the oven. Cook for a further 40 minutes.
To serve: Serve straight from the casserole, or transfer the chicken with the liquid and cabbage into a very large, warmed bowl or tureen. The chicken should be tender enough to be pulled apart with a pair of chopsticks. Serves four to six.

Basic red-cooked chicken

METRIC/IMPERIAL	AMERICAN
1 × 1½–2 kg/3–4 lb chicken	1 × 3–4 lb chicken
2 medium-sized onions	2 medium-sized onions
3–4 slices root ginger	3–4 slices root ginger
45–60 ml/3–4 tbsp vegetable oil	3–4 tbsp vegetable oil
75–90 ml/5–6 tbsp water	5–6 tbsp water
10 ml/2 tsp sugar	2 tsp sugar
75–90 ml/5–6 tbsp soya sauce	5–6 tbsp soy sauce
75–90 ml/5–6 tbsp dry sherry	5–6 tbsp dry sherry

To prepare: Cut the chicken into serving pieces. Chop each piece, through the bone, into three pieces. Slice the onions thinly. Peel and shred the ginger.
To cook: Heat the oil in a flameproof casserole over moderate heat. When the oil is hot, add the chicken pieces and stir-fry them for 3–4 minutes. Add the onions and ginger and stir-fry for 2–3 minutes. Sprinkle with water, sugar and soya sauce.

Stir and turn the chicken pieces in the sauce until they are well coated. Put the casserole into the oven preheated to 180°C (350°F) Gas Mark 4. Cook for 1 hour, stirring twice. Add the sherry, stir and return the casserole to the oven. Cook for a further 30 minutes.

To serve: Serve straight from the casserole, or transfer the chicken to a large, deep bowl or tureen. This is a dish with plenty of rich gravy, which is excellent to eat with rice. Serves four to six.

Red-cooked chicken with chestnuts

Repeat the recipe for Basic red-cooked chicken (page 42). Cook about 350 g/¾ lb of peeled chestnuts in boiling water for 30 minutes. Drain, then add to the chicken with an extra 25 ml/1½ tbsp of soya sauce at the same time as you add the sherry. Serves four to six.

Red-cooked chicken with bamboo shoots

Bamboo shoots are normally available canned; use about 100 g/¼ lb. Then drain off the can liquid and rinse bamboo shoots under cold running water. Cut into roughly the same size and shape as the chicken pieces. Repeat the recipe for Basic red-cooked chicken (page 42). Add the bamboo shoots to the casserole and mix with the chicken for the last 30 minutes of cooking time. Serves four to six.

Slow-simmered chicken (left)
Red-cooked chicken with chestnuts (below)

Paper-wrapped chicken

It is essential to use non-plastic cellophane paper, as the plastic-based kind will shrivel on contact with the hot oil.

METRIC/IMPERIAL	AMERICAN
4–5 Chinese dried mushrooms	4–5 Chinese dried mushrooms
1 boned chicken breast, weighing about 225 g/½ lb	1 boned chicken breast, weighing about ½ lb
4–5 broccoli spears	4–5 broccoli spears
3 spring onions	3 scallions
2 large pieces of cellophane paper	2 large pieces cellophane paper
2.5 ml/½ tsp salt	½ tsp salt
pepper	pepper
25 ml/1½ tbsp vegetable oil	1½ tbsp vegetable oil
15 ml/1 tbsp soya sauce	1 tbsp soy sauce
15 ml/1 tbsp hoisin sauce	1 tbsp hoisin sauce
15 ml/1 tbsp dry sherry	1 tbsp dry sherry
vegetable oil for deep-frying	vegetable oil for deep-frying

To prepare: Soak the dried mushrooms in 300 ml/½ pint (1¼ cups) of water for 30 minutes. Remove the stalks and cut the caps into thin strips. Cut the chicken meat into matchstick strips. Blanch the broccoli in boiling water for 1½ minutes. Drain and cut into similar-sized strips. Cut the spring onions (scallions) into 5 cm/2 in lengths. Cut the cellophane paper into 15 cm/5 in by 10 cm/4 in pieces. Rub the chicken all over with the salt, pepper, and oil. Leave for 30 minutes. Add all the vegetables and sprinkle with soya sauce, hoisin sauce and sherry. Rub the seasonings into the meat and vegetables. Place about 30 ml/2 tbsp of the mixture just below the middle of each piece of cellophane paper. Fold the bottom edge up to cover the ingredients and turn the two sides in. Finally, fold the top edge down and tuck in. Press each 'envelope' flat and pile them up as they are made. Place a light weight on top of every 4–5 envelopes to keep them firmly closed.

To cook: Heat the oil for deep-frying until it is very hot. Carefully lower 4–5 envelopes at a time into the oil and fry for 2½–3 minutes. Remove and drain on paper towels.

To serve: When all the stuffed envelopes have been fried, arrange them on a flat, warmed dish. The dishful of envelopes should give the appearance of lots of important and pleasant 'messages'. Before eating the contents, the diner should open each 'envelope' with the help of chopsticks. Since the food inside is enclosed and somewhat insulated it should still be quite hot when eaten, even after 4–5 minutes. This is a party or banquet dish. Serves four to six.

Lemon chicken

METRIC/IMPERIAL	AMERICAN
1 × 1½–2 kg/3–4 lb chicken	1 × 3–4 lb chicken
7.5 ml/1½ tsp salt	1½ tsp salt
pepper	pepper
75 ml/5 tbsp vegetable oil	5 tbsp vegetable oil
5–6 medium-sized Chinese dried mushrooms	5–6 medium-sized Chinese dried mushrooms
1 red pepper	1 red pepper
rind of 2 medium-sized lemons	rind of 2 medium-sized lemons
5 spring onions	5 scallions
4 slices root ginger	4 slices root ginger
15 ml/1 tbsp lard	1 tbsp lard
75 ml/5 tbsp clear broth (page 25)	5 tbsp clear broth (page 25)
60 ml/4 tbsp dry sherry	4 tbsp dry sherry
7.5 ml/1½ tsp sugar	1½ tsp sugar
30 ml/2 tbsp soya sauce (light coloured if available)	2 tbsp soy sauce (light coloured if available)
30–45 ml/2–3 tbsp fresh lemon juice	2–3 tbsp fresh lemon juice

To prepare: Cut the chicken into bite-sized pieces, discarding the bones. Rub all over with the salt, pepper and 25 ml/1½ tbsp of oil. Soak the dried mushrooms in 300 ml/½ pint (1¼ cups) of water for 30 minutes. Remove the stalks. Remove the pith and seeds from the pepper. Cut the lemon rind, pepper and dried mushrooms into matchstick strips. Cut the spring onions (scallions) into thin rounds. Peel and chop the ginger.

To cook: Heat the remaining oil in a large frying-pan over high heat. When the oil is very hot, add the chicken and stir-fry for 2 minutes. Remove the pieces from the pan and keep warm. Add the lard to the pan. When the fat has melted, add the ginger, pepper and mushrooms. Stir-fry for 1 minute. Add the lemon rind and spring onions (scallions). Stir-fry for ½ minute. Sprinkle with the broth, sherry, sugar and soya sauce. When the mixture boils, return the chicken to the pan. Stir in the sauce mixture for 1 minute. Sprinkle with lemon juice.

To serve: Turn into a warmed dish. Serves four to six.

Paper-wrapped chicken (left)
Lemon chicken (right)

Quick-fried chicken cubes in Peking soya paste sauce

METRIC/IMPERIAL	AMERICAN
2 boned chicken breasts, each weighing about 225 g/½ lb	2 boned chicken breasts, each weighing about ½ lb
25 ml/1½ tbsp cornflour	1½ tbsp cornstarch
60 ml/4 tbsp vegetable oil	4 tbsp vegetable oil
½ egg white	½ egg white
2 slices root ginger	2 slices root ginger
25 ml/1½ tbsp soya paste	1½ tbsp soy paste
10 ml/2 tsp soya sauce	2 tsp soy sauce
15 ml/1 tbsp hoisin sauce	1 tbsp hoisin sauce
7.5 ml/1½ tsp sugar	1½ tsp sugar
15 ml/1 tbsp lard	1 tbsp lard

To prepare: Cut the chicken meat into small cubes. Rub all over with the cornflour (cornstarch) and a quarter of the oil, and coat with the egg white. Peel and shred the ginger. Combine the soya paste, soya sauce, hoisin sauce and sugar.
To cook: Heat the remaining oil in a frying-pan over high heat. When the oil is hot, add the chicken cubes and ginger. Stir-fry for 1 minute. Push them to one side of the pan. Reduce the heat to moderate. Add the lard to the other side of the pan. When the fat has melted, add the sauce mixture. Stir in the fat until most of the moisture has evaporated and the sauce and fat are well blended. Mix the chicken cubes into the sauce. Stir and turn the chicken pieces until they are well coated.
To serve: Turn the chicken and sauce into a warmed dish.

Crispy skin chicken

METRIC/IMPERIAL	AMERICAN
3 slices root ginger	3 slices root ginger
17.5 ml/3½ tsp salt	3½ tsp salt
1 × 1½–2 kg/3–4 lb chicken	1 × 3–4 lb chicken

To prepare: Peel and shred the ginger and mix it with the salt. Blanch the chicken in boiling water for 3–4 minutes, skimming any scum from the surface. Leave to dry for 3–4 hours. When completely dry, rub all over with the salt/ginger mixture. Leave for 3–4 hours, or overnight.
To cook: Method 1 — put the chicken on a rack in a roasting pan. Put into the oven preheated to 190°C (375°F) Gas Mark 5. Roast for 1 hour, turning the chicken twice.
Method 2 — rub the chicken with a mixture of 5 ml/1 tsp of sugar mixed with 20 ml/1¼ tbsp of soya sauce and leave to dry thoroughly. Put the chicken in a deep-frying basket and deep-fry in hot oil until golden brown (about 7–8 minutes).
To serve: Cool the chicken slightly, then cut into serving pieces. Chop each piece through the bone into two or three. Arrange in a warmed dish which has been coated with 'salt and pepper dip' (a mixture of 1 part freshly ground black pepper with 4–5 parts of salt, heated together in a dry pan for 1½–2 minutes, stirring constantly). Serves four to six.

Stir-fried chicken livers with prawns (shrimps) and broccoli

METRIC/IMPERIAL	AMERICAN
350 g/¾ lb broccoli	2 cups broccoli
225 g/8 oz shelled prawns	8 oz shelled shrimps
5 ml/1 tsp salt	1 tsp salt
60 ml/4 tbsp vegetable oil	4 tbsp vegetable oil
225 g/8 oz chicken livers	8 oz chicken livers
25 ml/1½ tbsp soya sauce	1½ tbsp soy sauce
2 slices root ginger	2 slices root ginger
5 ml/1 tsp sugar	1 tsp sugar
30 ml/2 tbsp sherry	2 tbsp sherry

To prepare: Break the broccoli into small individual flowerets. Parboil for 3 minutes, then drain. Rub the prawns (shrimps) with salt and a quarter of the oil. Cut each liver into four pieces. Rub with half the soya sauce and another quarter of the oil. Peel and shred the ginger.
To cook: Heat the remaining oil in a frying-pan over high heat. When the oil is hot, add the ginger and stir-fry for ¼ minute. Add the prawns (shrimps) and chicken livers and stir-fry for 1½ minutes. Add the broccoli. Sprinkle with the sugar and sherry and bring to the boil. Sprinkle with the remaining soya sauce. Stir-fry for a further 2 minutes.
To serve: Turn into a warmed serving dish.

Quick-fried and braised soya chicken

METRIC/IMPERIAL	AMERICAN
4 cloves garlic	4 cloves garlic
3 slices root ginger	3 slices root ginger
1 × 1–1½ kg/2–3 lb chicken	1 × 2–3 lb chicken
7.5 ml/1½ tsp salt	1½ tsp salt
70 ml/4½ tbsp vegetable oil	4½ tbsp vegetable oil
60 ml/4 tbsp soya sauce	4 tbsp soy sauce
30 ml/2 tbsp hoisin sauce	2 tbsp hoisin sauce
10 ml/2 tsp sugar	2 tsp sugar
55 ml/3½ tbsp dry sherry	3½ tbsp dry sherry

To prepare: Crush the garlic. Peel and shred the ginger. Cut the chicken into serving pieces and chop each piece, through the bone, into three pieces. Rub the pieces all over with the salt, garlic, ginger and 25 ml/1½ tbsp of oil. Leave for 15 minutes.
To cook: Heat the remaining oil in a large frying-pan over high heat. When the oil is hot, add the chicken pieces. Stir-fry for 4–5 minutes. Add the soya sauce, hoisin sauce and sugar. Stir-fry for 2–3 minutes. Sprinkle with the sherry and stir and turn the pieces a few more times. Reduce the heat to low, cover the pan and cook very gently for a further 7–8 minutes. Uncover and stir and turn the chicken pieces a few times.
To serve: Transfer to a warmed dish.

Stir-fried chicken livers with prawns (shrimps) and broccoli

Duck Dishes

Salt-water duck

METRIC/IMPERIAL	AMERICAN
4–5 slices root ginger	4–5 slices root ginger
40 ml/2½ tbsp salt	2½ tbsp salt
7.5 ml/1½ tsp black pepper	1½ tsp black pepper
1 × 2–2½ kg/4–5 lb duck	1 × 4–5 lb duck

To prepare: Peel and finely chop the ginger. Mix with salt and pepper, and rub the mixture all over the duck, inside and out. Leave in the refrigerator for 1½ days.

To cook: Put the duck into a large saucepan. Cover with water and bring to the boil. Reduce the heat to low, cover the pan and simmer for 1¼ hours. Remove the duck and drain on paper towels.

To serve: Cut the duck into serving pieces. Chop each piece, through the bone, into 3–4 pieces. Arrange the pieces neatly using the backbone and rib-pieces as foundation. Arrange the leg and wing pieces around them, placing the breast meat on top. The bones are meant to be sucked for enjoyment. Accompany with rice or dry white wine. Serves four to six.

Braised and quick-fried duck with Chinese mushrooms and red pepper

METRIC/IMPERIAL	AMERICAN
225–350 g/½–¾ lb raw duck meat	½–¾ lb raw duck meat
30 ml/2 tbsp soya sauce	2 tbsp soy sauce
15 ml/1 tbsp soya paste	1 tbsp soy paste
15 ml/1 tbsp hoisin sauce	1 tbsp hoisin sauce
55 ml/3½ tbsp vegetable oil	3½ tbsp vegetable oil
8–10 medium-sized Chinese dried mushrooms	8–10 medium-sized Chinese dried mushrooms
1 red pepper	1 red pepper
15 ml/1 tbsp lard	1 tbsp lard
25 ml/1½ tbsp sherry	1½ tbsp sherry
5 ml/1 tsp sugar	1 tsp sugar
10 ml/2 tsp cornflour, mixed with 45 ml/3 tbsp clear broth (page 25)	2 tsp cornstarch, mixed with 3 tbsp clear broth (page 25)

To prepare: Cut the duck meat into 4 cm/1½ in pieces. Combine half the soya sauce, the soya paste, hoisin sauce and 15 ml/1 tbsp of oil until they are well blended. Rub over the duck meat and leave for 30 minutes. Soak the dried mushrooms in 300 ml/½ pint (1¼ cups) of water for 30 minutes. Remove the stalks and cut the caps in half. Remove the pith and seeds from the pepper and cut into 1.5 cm/½ in by 4 cm/1½ in strips.

To cook: Heat the remaining oil in a medium-sized frying-pan over high heat. When the oil is very hot, add the duck, and its marinade, and mushrooms. Stir-fry for 2½ minutes. Add the lard and pepper. Stir and turn with the duck meat for 1 minute. Add the sherry, remaining soya sauce, sugar and cornflour (cornstarch) mixture. Stir and turn for 1 minute. Reduce the heat to very low and simmer for 2–3 minutes.

To serve: Transfer to a warmed dish.

Onion and leek wine-simmered duck

METRIC/IMPERIAL	AMERICAN
6 medium-sized Chinese dried mushrooms	6 medium-sized Chinese dried mushrooms
1 × 2–2¼ kg/4–4½ lb duck	1 × 4–4½ lb duck
4 slices root ginger	4 slices root ginger
2 small leeks	2 small leeks
4 medium-sized onions	4 medium-sized onions
75 ml/5 tbsp vegetable oil	5 tbsp vegetable oil
5 ml/1 tsp salt	1 tsp salt
60 ml/4 tbsp soya sauce	4 tbsp soy sauce
900 ml/1½ pints water	3¾ cups water
300 ml/½ pint red wine	1¼ cups red wine
1 chicken stock cube	1 chicken stock cube

To prepare: Soak the dried mushrooms in 300 ml/½ pint (1¼ cups) of water for 30 minutes. Reserve the soaking water. Remove the stalks and cut the caps into quarters. Clean the duck under cold running water. Trim off any excess fat. Peel and chop the ginger. Clean the leeks thoroughly and cut into 5 cm/2 in lengths. Cut the onions in half. Fry the onions in the oil for 4–5 minutes and drain. Fry the duck in the same oil for 5–6 minutes until lightly browned. Stuff the cavity of the duck with the ginger, onions, salt and mushrooms.

To cook: Put the duck in a heavy-based saucepan or flameproof casserole. Add half the soya sauce and the water. Bring to the boil. Simmer gently for 45 minutes, turning over once. Leave to cool. When it is cold, skim off any scum from the surface. Discard two-thirds of the liquid. Add the wine, reserved mushroom soaking water, the remaining soya sauce and the crumbled stock cube. Bring to the boil. Simmer very gently for 1 hour, or until the liquid is reduced by half, turning the duck over twice. Remove the duck and arrange in a deep-sided, warmed dish. Keep hot. Add the leeks to the casserole. Increase the heat to high and boil rapidly until the liquid is reduced by half.

To serve: Spoon the sauce from the casserole over the duck and arrange the leeks around it. The duck should be tender enough to be pulled apart with a pair of chopsticks. Serves four to six.

Onion and leek wine-simmered duck

Crystal duck with chrysanthemums

Crystal duck with chrysanthemums is a duck in aspic but in China, pork skin is usually used as a jellifying agent. In the west, gelatine can be used as a substitute, as here. Chrysanthemums, in particular yellow ones, are often used in Chinese cooking.

METRIC/IMPERIAL	AMERICAN
1 × 1½–2 kg/3–4 lb duck	1 × 3–4 lb duck
4 slices root ginger	4 slices root ginger
2 medium-sized onions	2 medium-sized onions
3 spring onions	3 scallions
225 g/½ lb smoked ham	1⅓ cups smoked ham
1 large chrysanthemum	1 large chrysanthemum
15 ml/1 tbsp salt	1 tbsp salt
900 ml/1½ pints clear broth (page 25)	3¾ cups clear broth (page 25)
300 ml/½ pint white wine	1¼ cups white wine
1 small packet gelatine	1 small packet gelatin
8 small chrysanthemums	8 small chrysanthemums

To prepare: Clean the duck under cold running water. Chop, through the bone, into 12–15 pieces. Peel and chop the ginger. Cut the onions in half, the spring onions (scallions) into 5 cm/2 in lengths and the ham into similar-sized strips or lengths. Separate the petals from the large chrysanthemum.

To cook: Put the duck pieces into a flameproof casserole. Add the salt, ginger and onions. Pour in the broth and half the wine. Bring to the boil. Put the casserole into the oven preheated to 180°C (350°F) Gas Mark 4. Cook for 1½ hours, stirring every 30 minutes. Remove the casserole from the oven and discard the onion and ginger. Pour the liquid from the casserole into a separate pan, add the gelatine and stir until it has dissolved. Add the remaining wine. Skim off any scum from the surface and pour through fine muslin or cheesecloth to obtain a clear consommé. Arrange the duck pieces, skin side down, in a heatproof glass dish. Decorate with the spring onions (scallions), ham strips and chrysanthemum petals. Pour the consommé or broth over them. Place the dish in the oven to heat through for a further 15 minutes. Remove the dish from the oven. Leave to cool for 1 hour, then place in the refrigerator for 3–4 hours, or until the contents set.

To serve: When ready, turn the duck and jelly out on to a dish and decorate with the 8 small chrysanthemums. It can be further decorated by surrounding with suitable fruit and vegetables. Chinese shrimp sauce is sometimes served as a dip with this dish. Serves four to six.

Shredded duck quick-fried with shredded ginger

METRIC/IMPERIAL	AMERICAN
450 g/1 lb duck meat	1 lb duck meat
5–6 slices root ginger	5–6 slices root ginger
3 spring onions	3 scallions
2.5 ml/½ tsp salt	½ tsp salt
30 ml/2 tbsp soya sauce	2 tbsp soy sauce
15 ml/1 tbsp soya paste, or hoisin sauce	1 tbsp soya paste, or hoisin sauce
30 ml/2 tbsp dry sherry	2 tbsp dry sherry
40 ml/2½ tbsp vegetable oil	2½ tbsp vegetable oil
15 ml/1 tbsp lard	1 tbsp lard
15 ml/1 tbsp cornflour, mixed with 45 ml/3 tbsp water	1 tbsp cornstarch, mixed with 3 tbsp water

To prepare: Cut the duck meat into large matchstick shreds. Peel and cut the ginger diagonally into thin matchstick shreds. Cut the spring onions (scallions) into 4 cm/1½ in lengths. Combine the salt, soya sauce, soya paste, sherry and ginger and add to the duck meat. Stir and turn them until they are well blended. Leave for 30 minutes.

To cook: Heat the oil in a frying-pan over high heat. When the oil is hot, add the meat and ginger mixture. Stir-fry for 2 minutes. Add the lard. When the fat has melted, sprinkle over the spring onions (scallions) and cornflour (cornstarch) mixture. Stir and turn for 1 minute more.

To serve: Turn into a warmed dish. Serves four to six.

Crystal duck with chrysanthemums

Duck with almonds

Duck with almonds

METRIC/IMPERIAL	AMERICAN
450 g/1 lb duck meat	1 lb duck meat
2 slices root ginger	2 slices root ginger
5 ml/1 tsp salt	1 tsp salt
45 ml/3 tbsp vegetable oil	3 tbsp vegetable oil
2 spring onions	2 scallions
10 ml/2 tsp cornflour	2 tsp cornstarch
45 ml/3 tbsp stock	3 tbsp stock
30 ml/2 tbsp sherry	2 tbsp sherry
5 ml/1 tsp sugar	1 tsp sugar
40 ml/2 ½ tbsp soya sauce	2 ½ tbsp soy sauce
75 ml/5 tbsp green peas	5 tbsp green peas
75 ml/5 tbsp toasted almonds	5 tbsp toasted almonds

To prepare: Cut the duck meat into bite-sized pieces. Peel and shred the ginger, then mix with the salt. Rub the mixture into the duck with a third of the oil. Leave for 30 minutes. Cut the spring onions (scallions) into 1 cm/½ in lengths. Combine the cornflour (cornstarch), stock and sherry until they are well blended.

To cook: Heat the remaining oil in a frying-pan over high heat. Add the duck and spring onions (scallions) and stir-fry for 1½ minutes. Add the sugar and soya sauce and stir-fry for ½ minute. Add the peas and almonds. Stir-fry for a further 1 minute. Add the cornflour (cornstarch) mixture and stir until the sauce thickens. Simmer for a final ½ minute.

To serve: Turn into a warmed dish.

Beef and Lamb Dishes

Peking is sometimes called the 'mutton capital of China', which indicates just how popular that particular meat is there and in the north generally, although it is hardly eaten at all in the south. Both beef and lamb are the meats of the frontier regions — Manchuria, Mongolia and Sinkiang — where much of life is nomadic and there are large herds of cattle and sheep. Beef and lamb are often treated and cooked in similar ways in China, hence many of the recipes in this chapter can be made with either. The differences, if they exist, are that in the cooking of lamb or mutton, garlic is used as a seasoning, while beef is more often cooked with ginger. Also the tougher cuts of beef generally require about half as long again cooking time as lamb or mutton.

Red-cooked (or soya-braised) beef with broccoli

METRIC/IMPERIAL	AMERICAN
450 g/1 lb shin of beef	1 lb shin of beef
700 g/1 ½ lb brisket of beef	1 ½ lb brisket of beef
4–5 slices root ginger	4–5 slices root ginger
5 ml/1 tsp salt	1 tsp salt
2.5 ml/½ tsp peppercorns	½ tsp peppercorns
45 ml/3 tbsp soya sauce	3 tbsp soy sauce
600 ml/1 pint water	2 ½ cups water
300 ml/½ pint white wine	1 ¼ cups white wine
1 chicken stock cube	1 chicken stock cube
450 g/1 lb broccoli spears	1 lb broccoli spears

To prepare: Cut the beef into cubes. Blanch them in boiling water for 2 minutes and drain. Peel and chop the ginger.
To cook: Put the beef in a flameproof casserole. Add the ginger, salt, peppercorns, soya sauce and water. Bring to the boil. Put the casserole into the oven preheated to 180°C (350°F) Gas Mark 4. Cook for 2 hours, stirring a few times. Add the wine and crumbled stock cube. Return to the oven for a further 1 hour. Add broccoli and cook for a further 10 minutes.
To serve: Arrange the broccoli in a warmed dish and spoon the meat over. The soup from this dish is very clear broth which goes particularly well with rice. It is also excellent re-heated. Serves four to six.

Red-cooked (or soya-braised) mutton

Repeat the previous recipe, using 1–1¼ kg/2–2½ lb mutton instead of beef. Add 4–6 cloves of crushed garlic during the last hour of cooking.

Red-cooked (or soya-braised) beef with broccoli

Red-cooked (or soya-braised) oxtail

METRIC/IMPERIAL	AMERICAN
2–2½ kg/4–5 lb oxtail	4–5 lb oxtail
3–4 slices root ginger	3–4 slices root ginger
900 ml/1½ pints water	3¾ cups water
300 ml/½ pint red wine	1¼ cups red wine
3–4 slices root ginger	3–4 slices root ginger
5 ml/1 tsp salt	1 tsp salt
75 ml/5 tbsp soya sauce	5 tbsp soy sauce
10 ml/2 tsp sugar	2 tsp sugar
30 ml/2 tbsp tomato purée	2 tbsp tomato paste

To prepare: Chop (or get your butcher to chop) the oxtail into 7.5 cm/3 in lengths. Peel and chop the ginger.

To cook: Clean the oxtails thoroughly and put them into a flameproof casserole. Add all the other ingredients. Bring to the boil. Put the casserole into the oven preheated to 180°C (350°F) Gas Mark 4. Cook for 4 hours, stirring once every hour.

To serve: Serve straight from the casserole. The rich gravy from this dish is very good for eating with rice. After the long cooking, the meat should be easily detachable from the bones with chopsticks. The dish can also be re-heated when required. Serves four to six.

Simmered and deep-fried lamb

METRIC/IMPERIAL	AMERICAN
4 spring onions	4 scallions
¼ medium-sized cucumber	¼ medium-sized cucumber
3 slices root ginger	3 slices root ginger
700–900 g/1½–2 lb leg of lamb (in one piece)	1½–2 lb leg of lamb (in one piece)
vegetable oil for deep-frying	vegetable oil for deep-frying

Sauce	**Sauce**
25 ml/1½ tbsp soya sauce	1½ tbsp soy sauce
25 ml/1½ tbsp soya paste	1½ tbsp soy paste
25 ml/1½ tbsp hoisin sauce	1½ tbsp hoisin sauce
25 ml/1½ tbsp plum sauce	1½ tbsp plum sauce
25 ml/1½ tbsp dry sherry	1½ tbsp dry sherry
7.5 ml/1½ tsp sugar	1½ tsp sugar

To prepare: Cut the spring onions (scallions) into 4 cm/1½ in lengths. Cut the cucumber, lengthways, into similar matchstick strips. Peel and chop the ginger. Combine all the ingredients for the sauce until they are well blended.

To cook: Put the lamb in a flameproof casserole and cover with water. Bring to the boil, skimming any scum from the surface. Put the casserole into the oven preheated to 180°C (350°F) Gas Mark 4. Cook for 2½ hours, stirring a few times. Remove the lamb from the casserole. Reserve the cooking liquid for future use. Heat the oil in a deep-frying pan until it is very hot. Gently lower the lamb into the oil and fry for 8–9 minutes. Remove from the oil and drain on paper towels.

To serve: Cut the lamb while still hot into 1 cm/¼ in slices. Serve in toasted buns with cucumber, ginger and spring onions (scallions), accompanied by the sauce.

Stir-fried lambs' kidneys with celery and French (green) beans (above)
Simmered and deep-fried lamb (right)

Stir-fried lambs' kidneys with celery and French (green) beans

METRIC/IMPERIAL	AMERICAN
3–4 lambs' kidneys	3–4 lambs' kidneys
15 ml/1 tbsp soya paste, or hoisin sauce	1 tbsp soy paste, or hoisin sauce
25 ml/1½ tbsp soya sauce	1½ tbsp soy sauce
15 ml/1 tbsp vinegar	1 tbsp vinegar
45 ml/3 tbsp vegetable oil	3 tbsp vegetable oil
5 ml/1 tsp sugar	1 tsp sugar
½ chicken stock cube	½ chicken stock cube
90 ml/6 tbsp clear broth (page 25)	6 tbsp clear broth (page 25)
100 g/¼ lb French beans	⅔ cup green beans
2–3 stalks celery	2–3 stalks celery
15 ml/1 tbsp butter	1 tbsp butter

To prepare: Skin the kidneys and cut out the membrane and gristle. Cut each one into three strips. Score each strip with criss-cross cuts half-way through. Combine the soya paste, soya sauce, vinegar, a third of the oil and the sugar until they are well blended. Marinate the kidney strips in the sauce for 30 minutes. Dissolve the stock cube in the broth. Top and tail the French (green) beans. Cut the celery and beans into even-sized lengths.

To cook: Pour the broth into a saucepan. Add the celery, beans and butter. Stir-fry for 5 minutes over moderate heat. Heat the remaining oil in a frying-pan over high heat. When the oil is hot, pour in the kidney and marinade. Stir-fry for 1 minute. Push the kidney pieces to one side and pour the vegetables into the centre of the pan. When the contents come to the boil, stir-fry for a further ½ minute.

To serve: Transfer the mixture to a warmed dish. When you cook this dish, aim to produce the 'crisp-crunchiness' of the kidneys as well as preserve their unique flavour.

Stir-fried beef with celery and cabbage

METRIC/IMPERIAL	AMERICAN
½kg/1 lb rump steak	1 lb rump steak
2 slices root ginger	2 slices root ginger
5 ml/1 tsp sugar	1 tsp sugar
45 ml/3 tbsp soya sauce	3 tbsp soy sauce
60 ml/4 tbsp vegetable oil	4 tbsp vegetable oil
2 stalks celery	2 stalks celery
125–150 g/4–5 oz white or Chinese cabbage	4–5 oz white or Chinese cabbage
10 ml/2 tsp cornflour	2 tsp cornstarch
30 ml/2 tbsp stock or water	2 tbsp stock or water
30 ml/2 tbsp sherry	2 tbsp sherry

To prepare: Cut the steak into 5 cm/2 in by 2.5 cm/1 in slices. Peel and shred the ginger. Rub the beef with the ginger, sugar, 30 ml/2 tbsp of the soya sauce and a quarter of the oil. Leave for 10 minutes. Cut the celery diagonally into 2.5 cm/1 in lengths and the cabbage into similar pieces. Combine the cornflour (cornstarch), stock and sherry until they are well blended.
To cook: Heat the remaining oil in a large frying-pan over high heat. When the oil is very hot, add the beef, celery and cabbage. Stir-fry for 2½ minutes. Sprinkle with the remaining soya sauce and the cornflour (cornstarch) mixture and stir-fry for 1 minute, or until the sauce thickens.
To serve: Turn into a warmed dish.

Quick-fried beef with sweet peppers in black bean sauce

METRIC/IMPERIAL	AMERICAN
575–700 g/1¼–1½lb beef steak	1¼–1½lb beef steak
15 ml/1 tbsp soya sauce	1 tbsp soy sauce
15 ml/1 tbsp soya paste	1 tbsp soy paste
15 ml/1 tbsp hoisin sauce (optional)	1 tbsp hoisin sauce (optional)
15 ml/1 tbsp tomato purée	1 tbsp tomato paste
25 ml/1½ tbsp cornflour	1½ tbsp cornstarch
70 ml/4½ tbsp vegetable oil	4½ tbsp vegetable oil
6.5 ml/1¼ tsp sugar	1¼ tsp sugar
10 ml/2 tsp salted black beans	2 tsp salted black beans
2–3 slices root ginger	2–3 slices root ginger
1 medium-sized red pepper	1 medium-sized red pepper
1 medium-sized green pepper	1 medium-sized green pepper
45 ml/3 tbsp dry sherry	3 tbsp dry sherry

To prepare: Cut the beef into 4 cm/1½ in by 2.5 cm/1 in slices. Rub all over with soya sauce, soya paste, hoisin sauce, tomato purée (paste), cornflour (cornstarch), 15 ml/1 tbsp vegetable oil and the sugar. Leave for 15 minutes. Soak the black beans in water for 15 minutes. Peel and shred the ginger. Remove the pith and seeds from the peppers and cut them into 1.5 cm/½ in slices, then cut again into 4 cm/1½ in pieces.
To cook: Heat the remaining oil in a frying-pan over high heat. When the oil is hot, add the ginger and black beans. Stir-fry for ½ minute. Add the beef and stir-fry for 2 minutes. Add the peppers and sprinkle with the sherry. Stir-fry for a further 1 minute.
To serve: Turn on to a warmed dish.

Beef in clear broth with transparent noodles, cabbage, Chinese mushrooms and spring onions (scallions)

METRIC/IMPERIAL	AMERICAN
450 g/1 lb stewing steak	1 lb beef chuck
5–6 medium-sized Chinese dried mushrooms	5–6 medium-sized Chinese dried mushrooms
125 g/¼ lb transparent pea-starch noodles	¼ lb transparent pea-starch noodles
2 medium-sized carrots	2 medium-sized carrots
225 g/½lb cabbage or Chinese cabbage	2 cups cabbage or Chinese cabbage
2–3 spring onions	2–3 scallions
5 ml/1 tsp salt	1 tsp salt
2.5 ml/½ tsp peppercorns	½ tsp peppercorns
45 ml/3 tbsp soya sauce	3 tbsp soy sauce
600 ml/1 pint water	2½ cups water
300 ml/½ pint white wine	1¼ cups white wine
1 chicken stock cube	1 chicken stock cube
salt and pepper	salt and pepper

To prepare: Cut the beef into cubes. Blanch them in boiling water for 2 minutes and drain. Soak the dried mushrooms in 300 ml/½ pint (1¼ cups) of water for 30 minutes. Remove the stalks and cut the caps into quarters. Soak the noodles in hot water and then drain. Shred the carrots and cabbage. Cut the spring onions (scallions) into 2.5 cm/1 in lengths.
To cook: Put the beef into a flameproof casserole. Add the salt, peppercorns, soya sauce and water. Bring to the boil. Put the casserole into the oven preheated to 180°C (350°F) Gas Mark 4. Cook for 1 hour, stirring twice. Add the noodles, mushrooms and vegetables. Return to the oven and cook for 1 hour, stirring twice. Add the wine and crumbled stock cube and cook for a further 50 minutes. Sprinkle with spring onions (scallions) and season to taste. Return to the oven for a final 10 minutes.
To serve: Serve straight from the casserole.

Stir-fried beef with celery and cabbage

Shredded lamb stir-fried with transparent noodles and spring onions (scallions)

METRIC/IMPERIAL	AMERICAN
225 g/8 oz lean lamb	8 oz lean lamb
4–5 spring onions	4–5 scallions
1 egg	1 egg
15 ml/1 tbsp cornflour	1 tbsp cornstarch
125 g/4 oz transparent pea-starch noodles	4 oz transparent pea-starch noodles
1 chicken stock cube	1 chicken stock cube
300 ml/½ pint stock	1¼ cups stock
45 ml/3 tbsp vegetable oil	3 tbsp vegetable oil
30 ml/2 tbsp soya sauce	2 tbsp soy sauce
15 ml/1 tbsp sesame oil	1 tbsp sesame oil
30 ml/2 tbsp sherry	2 tbsp sherry

To prepare: Cut the lamb into thin strips. Cut the spring onions (scallions) into 5 cm/2 in lengths. Beat the egg lightly, then blend with the cornflour (cornstarch) and 25 ml/1½ tbsp of water into a batter. Add the lamb to the batter. Soak the noodles in hot water for 5 minutes. Dissolve the stock cube in the stock.

To cook: Heat the oil in a large frying-pan over high heat. Add the lamb and spread evenly over the pan. Stir-fry for 1 minute. Sprinkle with soya sauce and spring onions (scallions) and stir-fry for 1 minute. Add the stock and noodles and bring to the boil, stirring and turning to mix. Reduce the heat and simmer gently for 5 minutes. Sprinkle with the sesame oil and sherry. Simmer for a further 1 minute.

To serve: Turn into a warmed deep-sided dish. Serves four.

Quick-fried lamb with spring onions (scallions)

METRIC/IMPERIAL	AMERICAN
450–700 g/1–1½ lb leg of lamb	1–1½ lb leg of lamb
5 ml/1 tsp salt	1 tsp salt
pepper	pepper
30 ml/2 tbsp soya sauce	2 tbsp soy sauce
10 ml/2 tsp cornflour	2 tsp cornstarch
60 ml/4 tbsp vegetable oil	4 tbsp vegetable oil
4 cloves garlic	4 cloves garlic
5–6 spring onions	5–6 scallions
30 ml/2 tbsp dry sherry	2 tbsp dry sherry

To prepare: Cut the lamb into 4 cm/1½ in by 2.5 cm/1 in slices. Rub all over with the salt, pepper, soya sauce, cornflour (cornstarch) and a quarter of the oil. Crush the garlic and cut the spring onions (scallions) into 2.5 cm/1 in lengths.

To cook: Heat the remaining oil in a frying-pan over high heat. When the oil is hot, add the garlic and stir and turn in the oil once. Add the lamb and stir-fry for 2 minutes. Add the spring onions (scallions) and sherry. Stir-fry for 1 minute.

To serve: Turn on to a warmed dish.

Shredded lamb stir-fried with transparent noodles and spring onions (scallions) (above)
Beef meatballs with cabbage and celery (above right)

Quick-fried beef with spring onions (scallions)

Repeat Quick-fried lamb with spring onions (scallions) (left) but use beef (fillet or rump) instead of lamb. Add 4–5 slices of shredded root ginger in place of the garlic. (If you add 30 ml/2 tbsp of oyster sauce — or six fresh oysters — with the sherry, and prolong stir-frying for ½ minute, you will have Beef in oyster sauce, or Beef with oysters, two excellent and popular dishes from south-eastern China.)

Beef meatballs with cabbage and celery

METRIC/IMPERIAL	AMERICAN
2–3 water chestnuts (optional)	2–3 water chestnuts (optional)
350–450 g/¾–1 lb minced beef	¾–1 lb ground beef
2.5 ml/½ tsp salt	½ tsp salt
25 ml/1½ tbsp soya sauce	1½ tbsp soy sauce
15 ml/1 tbsp tomato purée	1 tbsp tomato paste
30 ml/2 tbsp cornflour	2 tbsp cornstarch
1 egg	1 egg
75 ml/5 tbsp vegetable oil	5 tbsp vegetable oil
1 medium-sized cabbage	1 medium-sized cabbage
2 stalks celery	2 stalks celery
½ chicken stock cube	½ chicken stock cube
150 ml/¼ pint hot clear broth (page 25)	⅝ cup hot clear broth (page 25)

To prepare: Shred the water chestnuts. Add them to the minced (ground) beef with the salt, soya sauce, tomato purée (paste), half the cornflour (cornstarch) and the egg. Form the mixture into 10–12 meatballs. Dust the meatballs with the remaining cornflour (cornstarch), then coat with 15 ml/1 tbsp of the oil. Cut the cabbage into 2.5 cm/1 in slices. Chop celery into 2.5 cm/1 in lengths. Dissolve the stock cube in the broth.

To cook: Heat the remaining oil in a frying-pan over moderate heat. When the oil is hot, add the meatballs. Cook the meatballs for 7–8 minutes, until evenly browned. Remove from the pan. Add the cabbage, celery and broth. Bring to the boil, turning the cabbage and celery in the broth, for 2–3 minutes. Transfer the cabbage and celery and broth to an ovenproof casserole. Arrange the meatballs on top of the cabbage and celery. Put the casserole into the oven preheated to 190°C (375°F) Gas Mark 5. Cook for 45 minutes.

To serve: Take to the table and serve the meatballs, vegetables and gravy straight from the casserole.

Spiced leg of lamb

METRIC/IMPERIAL	AMERICAN
1 × 2–2½ kg/4–5 lb leg of lamb	1 × 4–5 lb leg of lamb

Sauce | **Sauce**

6 garlic cloves	6 garlic cloves
6 slices root ginger	6 slices root ginger
2 medium-sized onions	2 medium-sized onions
1.25 L/2 pints stock	5 cups stock
75 ml/5 tbsp soya sauce	5 tbsp soy sauce
45 ml/3 tbsp soya paste or hoisin sauce	3 tbsp soy paste or hoisin sauce
10 ml/2 tsp dried chilli pepper or chilli sauce	2 tsp dried chilli pepper or chilli sauce
2.5 ml/½ tsp 5-spice powder	½ tsp 5-spice powder
30 ml/2 tbsp sugar	2 tbsp sugar
300 ml/½ pint red wine	1¼ cups red wine
1 chicken stock cube	1 chicken stock cube

To prepare: Crush the garlic and peel and shred the ginger. Slice the onions thinly. Add to the stock and combine with the other sauce ingredients until they are well blended. Pour the sauce into a saucepan and simmer gently for 45 minutes.

To cook: Put the leg of lamb into a large saucepan or flameproof casserole. Pour over the sauce mixture. Bring to the boil, then simmer gently for 1½ hours, turning over every 30 minutes. Set aside in the sauce to cool. Keep the lamb in the sauce, after it has cooled completely, for a further 3 hours (or overnight). About an hour before serving, place the lamb in a roasting pan and put into the oven preheated to 180°C (350°F) Gas Mark 4. Cook for 1 hour.

To serve: Slice the lamb into large bite-sized pieces and serve with dips such as plum sauce, hoisin sauce, Chinese soya-and-sherry mix or soya-and-vinegar mix. The lamb can also be eaten cold, with the same dips. Serves eight to ten.

Stir-fried lambs' liver with leeks and spring onions (scallions)

METRIC/IMPERIAL	AMERICAN
½ kg/1 lb lambs' liver	1 lb lambs' liver
30 ml/2 tbsp soya sauce	2 tbsp soy sauce
25 ml/1½ tbsp hoisin sauce	1½ tbsp hoisin sauce
5 ml/1 tsp sugar	1 tsp sugar
5 ml/1 tsp chilli sauce	1 tsp chilli sauce
45 ml/3 tbsp vegetable oil	3 tbsp vegetable oil
2 medium-sized leeks	2 medium-sized leeks
3 spring onions	3 scallions
15 ml/1 tbsp cornflour	1 tbsp cornstarch
30 ml/2 tbsp water	2 tbsp water
30 ml/2 tbsp dry sherry	2 tbsp dry sherry
15 ml/1 tbsp lard	1 tbsp lard

To prepare: Cut the liver into thin strips. Rub with half the soya sauce, hoisin sauce, sugar, chilli sauce and a third of the oil. Leave for 30 minutes. Clean the leeks thoroughly and cut the spring onions (scallions) and leeks into 2.5 cm/1 in lengths. Combine the cornflour (cornstarch), water and sherry.

To cook: Heat the remaining oil in a large frying-pan over high heat. When the oil is hot, add the leeks and stir-fry for 1 minute. Push to one side of the pan. Add the lard to the other side and, when it has melted, add the liver, spring onions (scallions), the remaining marinade, and the remaining soya sauce, hoisin sauce, sugar and chilli sauce. Stir-fry for a further 1½ minutes. Stir the leeks into the liver and spring onion (scallion) mixture for 1 minute. Sprinkle over the cornflour (cornstarch) mixture and stir until the sauce thickens.

To serve: Turn into a warmed dish. Serves four.

Spiced leg of lamb (below)
Stir-fried lambs' liver with leeks and spring onions (scallions) (right)

Egg Dishes

Eggs are used as extensively in China as anywhere else. In their natural shape they are most often seen as pickled eggs (known in the west as thousand year old eggs), salted eggs, tea eggs and soya braised eggs. When they are cooked with other ingredients — usually stir-fried, steamed or used as 'fu yung' (beaten egg white with one or more ingredients) — they can be made in any number of different combinations. They are most often stir-fried, perhaps because this is the quickest and easiest way to prepare and cook them. Although it might seem similar, a Chinese stir-fried egg dish is not exactly like a western omelette because the aim is not to wrap all the ingredients cooked inside a layer of 'set' egg, but to stir and turn the egg and any other ingredients lightly just before the top layer of the eggs has set completely. Thus in a well-cooked dish of stir-fried eggs, there should be a well-cooked layer of eggs (bottom layer next to the pan), mixed with the top layer which is slightly under-cooked. Chopped spring onions (scallions) and a dash of yellow wine (dry sherry) are often sprinkled over them to provide a characteristic and extremely appealing aroma.

Stir-fried eggs with shredded ham or bacon

METRIC/IMPERIAL	AMERICAN
4–5 eggs	4–5 eggs
5 ml/1 tsp salt	1 tsp salt
pepper	pepper
1–2 slices ham, or 2–3 rashers bacon	1–2 slices ham, or 2–3 slices bacon
3–4 spring onions	3–4 scallions
30 ml/2 tbsp vegetable oil	2 tbsp vegetable oil
30 ml/2 tbsp lard or butter	2 tbsp lard or butter
15 ml/1 tbsp dry sherry	1 tbsp dry sherry

To prepare: Break the eggs into a bowl. Sprinkle with the salt and a liberal amount of pepper, and beat until they are well blended. Cut the ham or bacon into matchstick strips. Cut the spring onions (scallions) into thin rounds.

To cook: Heat the oil and fat in a medium-sized frying-pan over moderate heat. When the fat has melted, add the ham or bacon and half the spring onions (scallions). Stir and spread evenly over the pan. Pour the beaten eggs into the pan, tilting the pan so they spread out evenly. Cook without stirring for 1 minute. Remove from the heat and leave until the eggs are just about to set. Then gently stir a few times. Return the pan to the heat. Sprinkle with the sherry and remaining spring onions (scallions). Cook until the mixture sizzles.

To serve: Turn on to a warmed dish and serve with a dishful of good-quality soya sauce, which is traditionally used as a dip. Simple as this dish is, it is marvellous — and filling to eat — with rice.

Stir-fried eggs with shrimps or crabmeat

Repeat Stir-fried eggs with shredded ham or bacon (above) using 75–90 ml/5–6 tbsp of shrimps or crabmeat, and 3 cloves of crushed garlic instead of ham and spring onions (scallions).

Steamed eggs with salt eggs, pickled eggs and quail eggs

METRIC/IMPERIAL	AMERICAN
2 eggs (chicken)	2 eggs (chicken)
5 ml/1 tsp salt	1 tsp salt
300 ml/½ pint clear broth (page 25)	1¼ cups clear broth (page 25)
2 salt eggs	2 salt eggs
2 pickled eggs	2 pickled eggs
4–5 quail eggs (optional)	4–5 quail eggs (optional)
20 ml/1¼ tbsp smoked ham	1¼ tbsp smoked ham
20 ml/1¼ tbsp spring onions	1¼ tbsp scallions

To prepare: Break the eggs into a bowl and beat until they are well blended. Add the salt and broth and stir until they are well blended. Remove the shells from the salt eggs and pickled eggs, and cut each into 6–8 segments. (Quail eggs are generally obtained from Chinese food shops canned and with the shells already removed.) Shred the ham and spring onions (scallions).

To cook: Arrange the salt egg and pickled egg segments alternately around the edge of a round or square deep-sided heatproof dish. Pour the broth mixture into the centre. Stand the quail eggs in the broth mixture. Put the dish into a steamer and steam for 10–12 minutes (or improvise by placing the dish on top of a bowl turned upside down in a large saucepan with a 2.5 cm/1 in layer of boiling water and boil for 10–12 minutes). Sprinkle the top of the quail eggs with the ham and beaten eggs with the spring onions (scallions). Steam for a further 3–4 minutes.

To serve: Remove the dish from the heat and serve from it. The different types of eggs in this dish provide a particularly intriguing mixture of flavours.

Tea eggs (Marbled eggs)

METRIC/IMPERIAL	AMERICAN
5–6 eggs	5–6 eggs
30 ml/2 tbsp Indian tea leaves	2 tbsp Indian tea leaves
30 ml/2 tbsp soya sauce	2 tbsp soy sauce

To prepare and cook: Hard-boil the eggs for 10–12 minutes. Crack the shells lightly with a spoon, but do not remove. Boil the tea leaves in 600 ml/1 pint (2½ cups) of water for 5–6 minutes, until the liquid is strong and dark. Add the soya sauce and stir. Sink the eggs into the liquid and leave for 1 hour, or until it is quite cool.

To serve: Remove the shells. You will find that some of the mixture has seeped through the shells to form a marble-like pattern on the whites. These eggs are usually served whole for picnics or midnight suppers. Allow one egg per person.

From top, clockwise: quail's eggs, painted egg shells, tea eggs, soya-braised eggs, salt eggs and thousand year old eggs

Steamed bean curd with egg yolks

METRIC/IMPERIAL	AMERICAN
2 cakes bean curd	2 cakes bean curd
2–3 egg yolks, or eggs	2–3 egg yolks, or eggs
7.5 ml/1½ tsp salt	1½ salt
½ chicken stock cube	½ chicken stock cube
150 ml/¼ pint hot clear broth (page 25)	⅝ cup hot clear broth (page 25)
15 ml/1 tbsp cornflour	1 tbsp cornstarch
30–45 ml/2–3 tbsp ham	2–3 tbsp ham
45 ml/3 tbsp Chinese snow pickles, or gherkins	3 tbsp Chinese snow pickles, or gherkins
45 ml/3 tbsp vegetable oil	3 tbsp vegetable oil
30 ml/2 tbsp lard or butter	2 tbsp lard or butter
45 ml/3 tbsp peas (shelled weight)	3 tbsp peas (shelled weight)

To prepare: Mash the bean curd. Break the eggs or egg yolks into a bowl. Sprinkle with salt and add the bean curd. Beat until they are well blended. Dissolve the stock cube in the broth. Add the cornflour (cornstarch). Add the mixture to the egg and bean-curd mixture. Beat until they are well blended. Chop the ham and pickles.

To cook: Heat the oil and fat in a saucepan over moderate heat. When the fat has melted, add the bean-curd mixture. When the centre starts to bubble, pour into a heatproof serving bowl. Sprinkle evenly with the chopped ham, pickles and peas. Put the bowl in a steamer and steam for 5–6 minutes (or improvise by placing the bowl in a large saucepan with about a 2.5 cm/1 in layer of boiling water, and boil for 5–6 minutes).

To serve: Remove the bowl from the heat and serve from it.

Mu-shu rou (yellow flower pork)

METRIC/IMPERIAL	AMERICAN
2–3 eggs	2–3 eggs
5 ml/1 tsp salt	1 tsp salt
5–6 medium-sized Chinese dried mushrooms	5–6 medium-sized Chinese dried mushrooms
30–45 ml/2–3 tbsp wood ears (optional)	2–3 tbsp wood ears (optional)
3 leeks	3 leeks
225 g/½ lb lean pork	½ lb lean pork

Steamed eggs with salt eggs, pickled eggs and quail eggs (page 62)

60 ml/4 tbsp vegetable oil   *4 tbsp vegetable oil*
30 ml/2 tbsp dry sherry   *2 tbsp dry sherry*
25 ml/1 ½ tbsp soya sauce   *1 ½ tbsp soy sauce*

To prepare: Break the eggs into a bowl. Sprinkle with the salt and beat until they are well blended. Soak the dried mushrooms in 300 ml/½ pint (1¼ cups) of water for 30 minutes. Remove the stalks and cut the caps into quarters. Soak the wood ears in water for 30 minutes. Drain and clean thoroughly. Clean the leeks thoroughly and cut them diagonally into 4 cm/1½ in lengths. Cut the pork into 4 cm/1½ in slices.

To cook: Heat the oil in a large frying-pan over high heat. When the oil is hot, add the pork. Sprinkle with salt and stir-fry for ½ minute. Push to one side of the pan. Add the mushrooms, leeks and wood ears. Stir-fry for 1 minute. Push them to the other side of the pan. Pour the beaten eggs into the centre of the pan. Remove the pan from the heat and leave until the eggs are set. Stir the contents of the pan together. Return the pan to the heat and sprinkle with the sherry. Cook for ½ minute. Sprinkle with soya sauce.

To serve: Turn on to a warmed dish. This is a favourite Pekingese dish, which is excellent with rice. It is also sometimes served wrapped in pancakes.

Steamed eggs

METRIC/IMPERIAL	AMERICAN
1 chicken stock cube	*1 chicken stock cube*
600 ml/1 pint hot clear broth (page 25)	*2 ½ cups hot clear broth (page 25)*
2 eggs	*2 eggs*
15 ml/1 tbsp spring onions	*1 tbsp scallions*
30 ml/2 tbsp smoked ham	*2 tbsp smoked ham*
25 ml/1 ½ tbsp soya sauce	*1 ½ tbsp soy sauce*

To prepare: Dissolve the stock cube in the broth. Leave to cool completely. Break the eggs into a bowl and beat until they are well blended. Add to the broth and mix thoroughly. Shred the spring onions (scallions) and ham.

To cook: Put the broth mixture into a heatproof bowl. Place the bowl in a steamer, and steam for 14–15 minutes (or improvise by placing the bowl in a large saucepan with a 2.5 cm/1 in layer of boiling water and boil for 14–15 minutes). Sprinkle the top of the broth mixture (which should now have set), with the chopped ham and spring onions (scallions), and steam for a further 5 minutes. Sprinkle with the soya sauce.

To serve: Remove the bowl from the heat and serve from it.

Mu-shu rou (yellow flower pork)

Shellfish

Shellfish are extremely popular in China, partly because they can be cooked quickly and partly because many of them, such as shrimps, clams, scallops and oysters, are the right size to be combined easily with numerous other ingredients. The large crustaceans such as lobsters and crabs can also be cooked quickly — either whole or chopped through their shells.

Steamed lobster I

Lobsters can usually be cooked in the same manner as crabs, but often they are steamed plain and eaten with dips.

METRIC/IMPERIAL	AMERICAN
3 cloves garlic	3 cloves garlic
1 × 1–1½kg/2–3 lb cooked lobster	1 × 2–3 lb cooked lobster
10 ml/2 tsp salt	2 tsp salt
2.5 ml/½ tsp MSG (optional)	½ tsp MSG (optional)
15 ml/1 tbsp dry sherry	1 tbsp dry sherry
15 ml/1 tbsp vegetable oil	1 tbsp vegetable oil
2 onions	2 onions

Dip	Dip
4–5 slices root ginger	4–5 slices root ginger
4 spring onions	4 scallions
15 ml/1 tbsp sugar	1 tbsp sugar
60 ml/4 tbsp soya sauce	4 tbsp soy sauce
60 ml/4 tbsp wine vinegar	4 tbsp wine vinegar
30 ml/2 tbsp dry sherry	2 tbsp dry sherry

To prepare: Crush the garlic. Cut the body of the lobster in half. Remove any black matter and spongy parts. Leave coral. Cut each half into three or four sections (depending on size). Rub all over with the salt, MSG, garlic, sherry and oil. Leave for 30 minutes. Slice the onions thinly. Peel and shred the ginger. Cut the spring onions (scallions) into 2.5 cm/1 in lengths. Combine all the dip ingredients until they are well blended. Pour into two small dishes.
To cook: Arrange the sliced onions over the bottom of a large heatproof dish. Top with the lobster pieces. Put the dish in a steamer and steam vigorously for 9–10 minutes (or improvise by placing the dish on a bowl turned upside down in a large saucepan with about a 2.5 cm/1 in layer of boiling water, and boil for 5–6 minutes).
To serve: Arrange the dishes containing the dips on each side of the main dish containing the lobster. In this dish the sauce is not cooked with the shellfish, so the diner has the choice of how much dip to apply.

Steamed lobster II

METRIC/IMPERIAL	AMERICAN
1 × 1–1½kg/2–3 lb cooked lobster	1 × 2–3 lb cooked lobster

Sauce	Sauce
3 cloves garlic	3 cloves garlic
2 slices root ginger	2 slices root ginger
2 spring onions	2 scallions
25 ml/1½ tbsp soya sauce	1½ tbsp soy sauce
25 ml/1½ tbsp hoisin sauce	1½ tbsp hoisin sauce
15 ml/1 tbsp vegetable oil	1 tbsp vegetable oil
5 ml/1 tsp chilli sauce	1 tsp chilli sauce
15 ml/1 tbsp sherry	1 tbsp sherry

To prepare: Prepare the lobster in the same way as Steamed lobster I. Crush the garlic and peel and shred the ginger. Shred the spring onions (scallions). Combine all the sauce ingredients until they are well blended. Arrange the lobster pieces, meat side up, on a heatproof dish. Sprinkle a little of the sauce mixture over the top of each piece.
To cook: Put the dish into a steamer and steam vigorously for 10 minutes (or improvise by placing the dish on a bowl turned upside down in a large saucepan with a 2.5 cm/1 in layer of boiling water, and boil for 10 minutes).
To serve: Turn the lobster pieces on to a warmed dish, and garnish with fresh vegetables such as watercress and parsley.

Black bean and ginger crab

METRIC/IMPERIAL	AMERICAN
2–3 medium-sized crabs	2–3 medium-sized crabs
4–5 slices root ginger	4–5 slices root ginger
10 ml/2 tsp salt	2 tsp salt
2 medium-sized onions	2 medium-sized onions
15 ml/1 tbsp salted black beans	1 tbsp salted black beans
15 ml/1 tbsp soya sauce	1 tbsp soy sauce
15 ml/1 tbsp chilli sauce	1 tbsp chilli sauce
30 ml/2 tbsp dry sherry	2 tbsp dry sherry
75 ml/5 tbsp clear broth (page 25)	5 tbsp clear broth (page 25)
75 ml/5 tbsp vegetable oil	5 tbsp vegetable oil

To prepare: Separate the large main shell from the body of each crab, by inserting a knife under the shell as a lever. Crack the claws and shells. Chop each body into quarters (leaving a leg or two attached to use as a 'handle' when eating). Scrape and remove all the spongy parts. Peel and shred the ginger. Rub all over the crab body with the salt and ginger. Slice the onions thinly. Soak the black beans in water for 30 minutes and drain. Combine the soya sauce, chilli sauce, sherry and broth until they are well blended.
To cook: Heat the oil in a large frying-pan over high heat. When the oil is hot, add the onions and black beans. Stir-fry for ½ minute. Add all the crab pieces. Stir-fry for 3–4 minutes, until well cooked through. Stir-fry for 3–4 minutes. Pour the broth sauce over the crab pieces and stir-fry them for a further 1½ minutes.
To serve: Turn the mixture on to a warmed dish. Eat by scraping the crabmeat (or crab-egg) out of the main shells, or holding on to one of the legs and chewing and sucking the meat out of the body. The mixture of crabmeat and the sauce in this dish produces a savouriness which is unsurpassed in Chinese cooking.

Onion and ginger crab with egg sauce

Repeat Black bean and ginger crab (above) using 4 cloves of crushed garlic for the black beans, and adding 3–4 spring onions (scallions) (cut into 2.5 cm/1 in lengths) into the mixture just before the broth sauce is added. The quantity of broth and soya sauce should be doubled, and 1 beaten egg should be dipped in a thin stream over the crab pieces just as the sauce is boiling and frothing up.

Onion and ginger crab with egg sauce

Butterfly deep-fried prawns (shrimps)

METRIC/IMPERIAL	AMERICAN
12–15 large/medium-sized prawns	12–15 large/medium-sized shrimps
15 ml/1 tbsp salt	1 tbsp salt

Batter

225 g/½ lb plain flour	2 cups all-purpose flour
300 ml/½ pint water	1¼ cups water
5 ml/1 tsp salt	1 tsp salt
10 ml/2 tsp baking powder	2 tsp baking powder
vegetable oil for deep-frying	vegetable oil for deep-frying

Quick-fried shrimps with chicken and mushrooms

METRIC/IMPERIAL	AMERICAN
1 boned chicken breast, weighing about 125 g/¼ lb	1 boned chicken breast, weighing about ¼ lb
¼ small cucumber	¼ small cucumber
15 ml/1 tbsp salt	1 tbsp salt
175 g/⅓ lb shrimps (shelled weight)	⅓ lb shrimps (shelled weight)
2 slices root ginger	2 slices root ginger
2 spring onions	2 scallions
30 ml/2 tbsp cornflour	2 tbsp cornstarch
45 ml/3 tbsp vegetable oil	3 tbsp vegetable oil
30 ml/2 tbsp lard or butter	2 tbsp lard or butter
125 g/¼ lb small button mushrooms	¾ cup small button mushrooms
	1½ tbsp soy sauce

To prepare: Remove the shells from the prawns (shrimps), leaving on the tails. Slice each prawn (shrimp) down the back to open up into a 'butterfly' shape. Rub the prawns (shrimps) all over with the salt. Leave for 30 minutes. Rinse quickly under cold running water and pat dry with paper towels. Combine all the batter ingredients until they are smooth and well blended.

To cook: Heat the oil in a deep-frying pan until it is very hot. Dip the prawns (shrimps), one at a time, into the batter, then drop carefully into the hot oil. Fry for 2½–3 minutes, until crisp and golden brown. Remove and drain on paper towels.

To serve: Transfer to a warmed dish. Serve hot with hoisin sauce and/or soya sauce with chilli sauce and tomato sauce added, as dips.

Butterfly deep-fried prawns (shrimps) (above) Crispy skin fish (right)

25 ml/1 ½ tbsp soya sauce
25 ml/1 ½ tbsp dry sherry
7.5 ml/1 ½ tsp sugar

1 ½ tbsp dry sherry
1 ½ tsp sugar

To prepare: Cut the chicken meat and cucumber into cubes. Dissolve the salt in 450 ml/¾ pint (2 cups) of water. Add the shrimps and soak for 30 minutes. Drain. Peel and chop the ginger. Shred the spring onions (scallions). Rub the shrimps and chicken cubes with the cornflour (cornstarch) and one-third of the oil.
To cook: Heat the remaining oil and fat in a large frying-pan over high heat. When the fat has melted, add the chicken and ginger. Stir-fry for ½ minute. Add the shrimps and mushrooms. Stir-fry for 1½ minutes. Add the soya sauce, sherry, sugar, spring onions (scallions) and cucumber. Stir-fry for a further 1 minute.
To serve: Turn on to a warmed dish.

Fish Dishes

Crispy skin fish

METRIC/IMPERIAL	AMERICAN
700 g/1½ lb medium-sized fish (whiting, herring, small trout, etc)	1½ lb medium-sized fish (whiting, herring, small trout, etc)
3–4 slices root ginger	3–4 slices root ginger
15 ml/1 tbsp salt	1 tbsp salt
25 ml/1½ tbsp flour	1½ tbsp flour
oil for deep-frying	oil for deep-frying

To prepare: Gut and clean the fish thoroughly (you can ask your fishmonger to do this). Peel and chop the ginger, then mix with the salt. Rub the mixture over the fish, inside and outside, and leave for 3 hours. Rub with flour and leave for a further 30 minutes.
To cook: Heat the oil in a deep-frying pan until it is very hot. Arrange half the fish in a deep-frying basket and carefully lower into the oil. Fry for 3–4 minutes, or until the fish are crisp and golden brown. Remove from the oil and dry on paper towels. Keep hot while you fry the remaining fish in the same way. When the fish has been drained thoroughly, return them to the oil for a second frying, for 2½–3 minutes, or until very crisp — even the bones and heads should be crisp enough to eat.
To serve: Transfer to a warmed dish and eat with plain rice. The contrast between the salty-brittle crispiness of the fish and the rice makes this a good combination. Serves four to six.

Fish simmered in clear broth

METRIC/IMPERIAL	AMERICAN
1 × ½–1 kg/1–2 lb whole fish (carp, mullet, bream, trout, etc)	1 × 1–2 lb whole fish (carp, mullet, bream, trout, etc)
10 ml/2 tsp salt	2 tsp salt
3 medium-sized Chinese dried mushrooms	3 medium-sized Chinese dried mushrooms
3 spring onions	3 scallions
2 rashers streaky bacon	2 slices fatty bacon
3 slices root ginger	3 slices root ginger
450 ml/¾ pint clear broth (page 25)	2 cups clear broth (page 25)
30 ml/2 tbsp wine vinegar	2 tbsp wine vinegar
30 ml/2 tbsp sherry	2 tbsp sherry
½ chicken stock cube	½ chicken stock cube

To prepare: Rub the fish, inside and out, with salt and leave for 1 hour. Soak the dried mushrooms in 300 ml/½ pint (1¼ cups) of water for 30 minutes. Discard the stalks and cut the caps into matchstick strips. Cut the spring onions (scallions) into 5 cm/2 in lengths. Cut the bacon, across the lean and fat, into matchstick strips. Peel and shred the ginger.
To cook: Put the fish in an oval or rectangular flameproof casserole. Gently pour over the broth. Add the vinegar and sherry and sprinkle with the crumbled stock cube. Decorate the top of the fish with the bacon, ginger, spring onions (scallions) and mushrooms. Cover the casserole and put it into the oven preheated to 190°C (375°F) Gas Mark 5. Cook for 35 minutes.
To serve: Serve straight from the casserole. This is another 'semi-soup' dish, where the cooking broth is drunk with rice.

Baked red-cooked (or soya-braised) fish

METRIC/IMPERIAL	AMERICAN
450–700 g/1–1½lb fish (cod, haddock, carp, bream, etc)	1–1½lb fish, (cod, haddock, carp, bream, etc)
2 slices root ginger	2 slices root ginger
5 ml/1 tsp salt	1 tsp salt
15 ml/1 tbsp soya sauce	1 tbsp soy sauce
15 ml/1 tbsp hoisin sauce	1 tbsp hoisin sauce
25 ml/1½ tbsp cornflour	1½ tbsp cornstarch
25 ml/1½ tbsp vegetable oil	1½ tbsp vegetable oil

Sauce and garnish	**Sauce and garnish**
3 spring onions	3 scallions
25 ml/1½ tbsp lard	1½ tbsp lard
25 ml/1½ tbsp soya sauce	1½ tbsp soy sauce
25 ml/1½ tbsp wine vinegar	1½ tbsp wine vinegar
25 ml/1½ tbsp sherry	1½ tbsp sherry
7.5 ml/1½ tsp sugar	1½ tsp sugar

To prepare: Cut the fish into 5–6 pieces and arrange in a roasting pan. Peel and chop the ginger. Rub the fish with the ginger, salt, soya sauce, hoisin sauce, cornflour (cornstarch) and oil. Leave for 30 minutes. Cut the spring onions (scallions) into 4 cm/1½ in lengths.

To cook: Put the roasting pan into the oven preheated to 220°C (425°F) Gas Mark 7. Roast for 10–12 minutes. Remove the fish pieces from the pan and arrange on a warmed serving dish. Set the roasting pan over moderate heat. Add the lard, spring onions (scallions), soya sauce, vinegar, sherry and sugar. Stir and boil for ½ minute. Pour over the fish pieces in the serving dish.

To serve: Bring the serving dish to the table.

Steamed five willow fish

METRIC/IMPERIAL	AMERICAN
1 × ¾–1 kg/1½–2 lb whole fish (trout, bream, carp, mullet, salmon, etc)	1 × 1½–2 lb whole fish (trout, bream, carp, mullet, salmon, etc)
10 ml/2 tsp salt	2 tsp salt
25 ml/1½ tbsp vegetable oil	1½ tbsp vegetable oil
6 spring onions	6 scallions
6 slices root ginger	6 slices root ginger
1 red pepper	1 red pepper
2–3 pieces bamboo shoot	2–3 pieces bamboo shoot
2 small chilli peppers	2 small chilli peppers
45 ml/3 tbsp lard	3 tbsp lard
45 ml/3 tbsp soya sauce	3 tbsp soy sauce
45 ml/3 tbsp wine vinegar	3 tbsp wine vinegar
15 ml/1 tbsp cornflour, mixed with 75 ml/5 tbsp clear broth (page 25)	1 tbsp cornstarch, mixed with 5 tbsp clear broth (page 25)

To prepare: Rub the fish, inside and out, with the salt and oil, and leave for 30 minutes. Cut the spring onions (scallions) into 5 cm/2 in lengths. Peel and shred the ginger. Remove and discard the seeds and pith from the pepper and shred. Shred the bamboo shoot. Shred the chilli peppers, discarding the pips.

To cook: Arrange the fish in an oval heatproof serving dish and place the dish in a steamer. Steam vigorously for 15 minutes. Heat the lard in a frying-pan over moderate heat. When the fat has melted, add the chilli peppers and stir and turn in the hot fat a few times. Add all the vegetables, soya sauce and vinegar and stir-fry for 15 seconds. Add the cornflour (cornstarch) mixture and stir until the sauce thickens.

To serve: Garnish the fish with the solid ingredients from the frying-pan, and pour the sauce over the fish. The strong flavour of the sauce and garnish brings out the juicy freshness of the fish.

Sweet and sour whole fish

Repeat Steamed five willow fish (above). Add 25 ml/1½ tbsp of sugar, the same quantity of tomato purée (paste), and twice the quantity of orange juice to the sauce when adding the soya sauce and vinegar. Sweet and sour whole fish can also be cooked by deep-frying the fish after an initial seasoning, for about 7–8 minutes, or until crispy. The sauce, prepared in the same way as above, is poured over the fish just before serving.

Steamed five willow fish (left)
Sweet and sour whole fish (right)

Vegetable Dishes

What seems to make Chinese vegetable dishes more flavoursome than those of many other cuisines is that much of the time they are cooked in their own juices, either by quick stir-frying (where only a small amount of oil is added), or by slow-braising where some clear broth, meat juices or gravies and soya sauce are added.

Sweet and sour cabbage

METRIC/IMPERIAL	AMERICAN
1 Chinese or Savoy cabbage	1 Chinese or Savoy cabbage
45 ml/3 tbsp vegetable oil	3 tbsp vegetable oil
15 ml/1 tbsp butter	1 tbsp butter
5 ml/1 tsp salt	1 tsp salt

Sauce	**Sauce**
25 ml/1½ tbsp cornflour	1½ tbsp cornstarch
75 ml/5 tbsp water	5 tbsp water
25 ml/1½ tbsp soya sauce	1½ tbsp soy sauce
40 ml/2½ tbsp sugar	2½ tbsp sugar
55 ml/3½ tbsp vinegar	3½ tbsp vinegar
55 ml/3½ tbsp orange juice	3½ tbsp orange juice
40 ml/2½ tbsp tomato purée	2½ tbsp tomato paste
25 ml/1½ tbsp sherry	1½ tbsp sherry

To prepare: Clean, then shred the cabbage into thin slices. Combine all the sauce ingredients until they are well blended.

To cook: Heat the oil and butter in a large saucepan over high heat. When the oil is hot, add the cabbage and sprinkle with salt. Stir-fry for 2 minutes. Reduce the heat to low and simmer gently for 5–6 minutes. Put the sauce mixture into a small saucepan and simmer for 4–5 minutes, stirring constantly, until the liquid thickens and becomes translucent.

To serve: Turn out the cabbage on to a warmed deep-sided dish or bowl and pour over the sauce. Serves four to six.

Hot-tossed stir-fried mixed vegetables

METRIC/IMPERIAL	AMERICAN
2 slices root ginger	2 slices root ginger
3 cloves garlic	3 cloves garlic
1 medium-sized onion	1 medium-sized onion
½ green pepper	½ green pepper
½ red pepper	½ red pepper
¼ medium-sized cucumber	¼ medium-sized cucumber
2 stalks celery	2 stalks celery
2 spring onions	2 scallions
3–4 lettuce leaves	3–4 lettuce leaves
¼ chicken stock cube	¼ chicken stock cube
30 ml/2 tbsp hot clear broth (page 25)	2 tbsp hot clear broth (page 25)
55 ml/3½ tbsp vegetable oil	3½ tbsp vegetable oil
7.5 ml/1½ tsp salt	1½ tsp salt
225 g/½lb bean sprouts	1⅓ cups bean sprouts
7.5 ml/1½ tsp sugar	1½ tsp sugar
30 ml/2 tbsp soya sauce	2 tbsp soy sauce
15 ml/1 tbsp lemon juice	1 tbsp lemon juice
15 ml/1 tbsp sesame oil	1 tbsp sesame oil

To prepare: Peel and shred the ginger, crush the garlic and cut the onion into thin slices, then separate into rings. Remove the pith and seeds from the peppers and cut them and the cucumber into matchstick strips. Cut the celery and spring onions diagonally into 4cm/1½in lengths. Chop the lettuce. Dissolve the stock cube in the broth.

To cook: Heat the oil in a large frying-pan over moderate heat. When the oil is hot, add the onion, ginger, garlic and salt. Stir-fry for ½ minute. Add all the other vegetables. Increase the heat to high and stir and turn the vegetables in the oil until they are all well coated. Sprinkle with sugar, soya sauce and chicken stock. Stir-fry for 1½ minutes. Sprinkle with lemon juice and sesame oil, and turn once more.

To serve: Turn into a warmed dish and serve as a 'hot salad'.

Sweet and sour cabbage (below)

Hot-tossed stir-fried mixed vegetables (right)

Red-cooked (or soya-braised) cabbage

METRIC/IMPERIAL	AMERICAN
1 medium-sized cabbage	1 medium-sized cabbage
½ chicken stock cube	½ chicken stock cube
75–90 ml/5–6 tbsp hot water	5–6 tbsp hot water
30 ml/2 tbsp soya sauce	2 tbsp soy sauce
7.5 ml/1½ tsp sugar	1½ tsp sugar
pepper	pepper
40 ml/2½ tbsp vegetable oil	2½ tbsp vegetable oil
25 ml/1½ tbsp lard or butter	1½ tbsp lard or butter

To prepare: Cut the cabbage into 2.5 cm/1 in slices, discarding the tougher parts of the stem. Dissolve the stock cube in the hot water. Combine the soya sauce, chicken stock, sugar and pepper until they are well blended.

To cook: Heat the oil and fat in a saucepan over moderate heat. When the fat has melted, add the cabbage and stir and turn in the hot fat until it is well coated. Sprinkle the soya sauce mixture evenly over the cabbage, and stir around several times. Reduce the heat to very low, cover and simmer for 18–20 minutes, stirring every 4–5 minutes.

To serve: Turn on to a warmed dish. The cabbage should be tender, but still crisp. Most semi-hard vegetables can be cooked in this way, for shorter or longer times as appropriate.

Cauliflower fu-yung

METRIC/IMPERIAL	AMERICAN
1 large cauliflower	1 large cauliflower
½ chicken stock cube	½ chicken stock cube
150 ml/¼ pint hot clear broth (page 25)	⅝ cup hot clear broth (page 25)

Fu-Yung

	Fu-Yung
3 egg whites	3 egg whites
45–60 ml/3–4 tbsp minced chicken breast	3–4 tbsp ground chicken breast
5 ml/1 tsp salt	1 tsp salt
pepper	pepper
30 ml/2 tbsp milk	2 tbsp milk
30 ml/2 tbsp cornflour	2 tbsp cornstarch
30 ml/2 tbsp vegetable oil	2 tbsp vegetable oil
30 ml/2 tbsp butter	2 tbsp butter

To prepare: Divide the cauliflower into very small flowerets. Beat the egg whites, minced (ground) chicken, salt, pepper, milk and cornflour (cornstarch) together until the mixture is nearly stiff but not dry. Dissolve the stock cube in the broth.
To cook: Heat the broth in a large saucepan over moderate heat. Add the cauliflower pieces and stir and turn them for 3–4 minutes, until the liquid has almost evaporated. Heat the oil and fat in a large frying-pan over moderately low heat. When the fat has melted, add the beaten egg white mixture. Turn it in the fat for 1 minute. Pour in the cauliflower pieces and increase the heat to high. Stir and turn the cauliflower in the egg white mixture for 1½–2 minutes, until well covered.
To serve: Turn on to a warmed dish. Occasionally in China some minced (ground) ham or crabmeat is sprinkled over the contents of this dish, for additional colour and flavour.

Broccoli fu-yung

Repeat Cauliflower fu-yung, (above) using broccoli instead of cauliflower.

Hot quick-fried spinach

METRIC/IMPERIAL	AMERICAN
450 g/1 lb spinach	4 cups spinach
3–4 cloves garlic	3–4 cloves garlic
45 ml/3 tbsp vegetable oil	3 tbsp vegetable oil
30 ml/2 tbsp butter	2 tbsp butter
5 ml/1 tsp salt	1 tsp salt

Quick-fried French (green) beans in onion and garlic sauce

METRIC/IMPERIAL	AMERICAN
15 ml/1 tbsp soya sauce	1 tbsp soy sauce
5 ml/1 tsp sugar	1 tsp sugar
15 ml/1 tbsp dry sherry	1 tbsp dry sherry
15 ml/1 tbsp lard	1 tbsp lard

To prepare: Clean the spinach thoroughly and trim. Pat dry thoroughly. Crush the garlic.

To cook: Heat the oil and fat in a large saucepan. When the fat has melted, add the salt and garlic. Stir and turn them in the hot fat a few times. Pour in the spinach and increase the heat to high. Stir and turn quickly in the fat until every leaf is well coated, for 2 minutes. Sprinkle with soya sauce, sugar and sherry. Stir-fry for 1 minute. Add the lard to give the spinach a final 'gloss' and stir-fry in the melting fat a few times.

To serve: Turn on to a warmed dish. This may seem a rough and ready dish, but it is brilliantly colourful and highly delectable to eat.

Quick-fried French (green) beans in onion and garlic sauce

METRIC/IMPERIAL	AMERICAN
450 g/1 lb French beans	2 ²/₃ cups green beans
½ chicken stock cube	½ chicken stock cube
150 ml/¼ pint hot clear broth (page 25)	⅝ cup hot clear broth (page 25)
4–6 cloves garlic	4–6 cloves garlic
2 spring onions	2 scallions
45 ml/3 tbsp vegetable oil	3 tbsp vegetable oil
25 ml/1 ½ tbsp butter	1 ½ tbsp butter
5 ml/1 tsp salt	1 tsp salt
15 ml/1 tbsp soya sauce	1 tbsp soy sauce
5 ml/1 tsp sugar	1 tsp sugar
15 ml/1 tbsp dry sherry	1 tbsp dry sherry

To prepare: Top and tail the beans. Dissolve the stock cube in the broth. Crush the garlic and cut the spring onions (scallions) into thin rounds.

To cook: Heat the broth in a large saucepan. Add the beans and simmer until nearly all the liquid has evaporated, turning them constantly. Heat the oil and fat in a large frying-pan over moderate heat. Add the garlic, salt and spring onions (scallions). Stir and turn them in the hot fat for ½ minute. Add the beans and stir and turn them in the fat until they are well coated. Sprinkle with soya sauce, sugar and sherry. Stir-fry for a further 1 minute.

To serve: Turn on to a warmed dish. This is an excellent dish to accompany rice and meat.

Sweet Dishes

Steamed honeyed pears

METRIC/IMPERIAL	AMERICAN
4 medium-sized or large pears	*4 medium-sized or large pears*
60 ml/4 tbsp sugar	*4 tbsp sugar*
60 ml/4 tbsp clear honey	*4 tbsp clear honey*
30 ml/2 tbsp sweet liqueur (Chinese 'rose dew', cherry brandy or crème de menthe)	*2 tbsp sweet liqueur (Chinese 'rose dew', cherry brandy or crème de menthe)*

To prepare: Peel the pears, leaving the stem and about 1 cm/¼ in of surrounding skin for ease in handling.

To cook: Stand the pears in a saucepan and just cover with water. Bring to the boil over low heat and simmer for 30 minutes. Pour off half the water. Sprinkle the pears with the sugar and simmer for a further 10 minutes. Remove the pears from the pan and chill in the refrigerator for 2 hours. Meanwhile, pour off a further half of the water in the pan. Add the honey and liqueur to the water and stir until they are well blended. Put the mixture into the refrigerator with the pears for the 2 hours.

To serve: Arrange the pears in individual dessert dishes. Pour the honey mixture over them and serve. This is a refreshing dessert to serve in summer, or after several courses of hot savoury food. Allow one pear per person.

Eight precious rice pudding (below)
Steamed honeyed pears (right)

Eight precious rice pudding

METRIC/IMPERIAL	AMERICAN
700 g/1 ½lb glutinous rice	*4 cups glutinous rice*
60–75 ml/4–5 tbsp lard	*4–5 tbsp lard*
120 ml/8 tbsp candied fruit (dried lichees, dates, raisins, preserved ginger, prunes, cherries and mixed fruit)	*8 tbsp candied fruit (dried lichees, dates, raisins, preserved ginger, prunes, cherries and mixed fruit)*
60–75 ml/4–5 tbsp nuts (almonds, chestnuts, walnuts, melon seeds, etc)	*4–5 tbsp nuts (almonds, chestnuts, walnuts, melon seeds, etc)*
75 ml/5 tbsp sugar	*5 tbsp sugar*
105–120 ml/7–8 tbsp sweetened bean curd cheese or date purée	*7–8 tbsp sweetened bean curd cheese or date purée*

To prepare: Cook the rice as for Basic boiled rice (page 12). Grease a heatproof basin generously with two-thirds of the lard. Stick the candied fruit and nuts in the lard, pushing them against the sides, and arrange the remainder at the bottom. Add the sugar and remaining lard to the rice and mix well. Spoon half the rice into the basin, levelling off the top. Spoon the sweetened bean paste on top of the rice, then cover the paste with the remaining rice, leaving about 1.5 cm/½ in space at the top of the basin.

To cook: Seal the top of the basin with a cloth or foil, and place it in a steamer. Steam for 1½ hours (or improvise by placing the bowl in a large saucepan with a 2.5 cm/1in layer of boiling water, and boil for 1½ hours).

To serve: Remove the basin from the steamer and remove the cloth or foil. Invert the basin on to a dish, shaking the pudding out in one piece. The colourful fruits and nuts and the layer of brown sweetened bean paste make a colourful dish. Serves four to six.

Caramel apples

METRIC/IMPERIAL
6 medium-sized apples
90 ml/6 tbsp plain flour
15 ml/1 tbsp cornflour
2 egg whites
vegetable oil for deep-frying
125 g/4 oz sugar
15 ml/1 tbsp sesame seeds
15 ml/1 tbsp vegetable oil

AMERICAN
6 medium-sized apples
6 tbsp all-purpose flour
1 tbsp cornstarch
2 egg whites
vegetable oil for deep-frying
½ cup sugar
1 tbsp sesame seeds
1 tbsp vegetable oil

To prepare: Peel, core and quarter the apples. Dust the apple quarters lightly with a little of the plain (all-purpose) flour. Sift the remaining flour and cornflour (cornstarch) together, add the egg whites and mix to a paste.

To cook: Heat the oil in a deep-frying pan until it is hot. Coat

the apple quarters, one at a time, in the paste, then drop carefully into the oil. Fry until golden brown. Remove and drain on paper towels. Place the sugar in a small saucepan with 30 ml/2 tbsp water. Heat, stirring, until the sugar has caramelised and is a light golden brown. Stir in the apple quarters and sesame seeds.

To serve: Serve in individual, lightly oiled serving dishes. A bowl of cold water could also be on the table, so that diners can pick up their apple with chopsticks and lower them into the water before eating, to harden the caramel. Serves four to six.

Almond jelly with chow chow

METRIC/IMPERIAL	AMERICAN
60 ml/4 tbsp gelatine	4 tbsp gelatin
450 ml/¾ pint water	2 cups water
450 ml/¾ pint milk	2 cups milk
55 ml/3½ tbsp sugar	3½ tbsp sugar
5 ml/1 tsp almond essence	1 tsp almond extract
1 large or 2 small cans chow chow	1 large or 2 small cans chow chow

To prepare: Soften the gelatine in one-quarter of the water, in a heatproof bowl placed over a saucepan of hot water. Stir until the gelatine has dissolved. Heat the remaining water with the milk, sugar and almond essence (extract), stirring until all the solids have dissolved. Stir in the gelatine for 1 minute. Pour the mixture into a lightly oiled rectangular pan and leave until cooled and set.

To serve: Cut the almond jelly into triangular or rectangular bite-sized pieces. Arrange in a large bowl and pour the chow chow into the centre. Chill before serving.

Chilled melon bowl

METRIC/IMPERIAL	AMERICAN
1 large melon or watermelon	1 large melon or watermelon
1 small tin lichees (in syrup)	1 small can lichees (in syrup)
60–75 ml/4–5 tbsp preserved ginger	4–5 tbsp preserved ginger (optional)
any mixture of fresh and tinned fruit (pineapple, strawberries, pears, etc)	any mixture of fresh and canned fruit (pineapple, strawberries, pears, etc)

To prepare: Slice 5 cm/2 in from the top of the melon. Remove the seeds and scoop out the inside carefully, in large pieces. Cut into even-sized pieces. Mix melon pieces with the other fruits, which have been cut into similar-sized pieces. Fill the cavity of the melon with this fruit salad. Chill in the refrigerator for 2–3 hours.

To serve: Remove from the refrigerator and top with a piece (or several pieces) of ice. Serve the chilled fruit salad from the melon shell. One large melon will serve four to six, and one watermelon about six to eight.

Caramel apples (far left)
Almond jelly with chow chow (left)

Regional cooking

All regional cooking in China evolved to a great extent from the geography and history of the regions concerned. Almost every province (they are roughly equivalent to a state in the United States), has dishes of its own, but since there are over twenty of these provinces, it would be over-complicating the situation unnecessarily to accord a 'cuisine' to each one. There is a cookery book, published in China, which divides regional cooking into eleven types, but as the character of many regions overlap, it is now more usual to divide the country gastronomically into four main sections, Peking and North China cooking, Shanghai and East China cooking, Canton and South China cooking, and Szechuan and West China cooking. If you can differentiate these styles clearly, you will have achieved a clearer understanding of the nature of Chinese food than most of the Chinese themselves — and this includes most Chinese restaurateurs!

Peking and North China cooking

North China, where Peking is situated, stretches to the borders of Inner Mongolia where the land is arid but where, nevertheless, great grasslands stretch for more than a thousand miles to the east and west. It is therefore not surprising that the cooking of this region reflects a continental character; much meat is consumed (especially lamb and mutton) and a good deal of the cooking is simple — roasting, deep-boiling and barbecuing. Where there are refinements, they come usually in the form of strong-tasting 'dips' for the meat. Strong-tasting vegetables, such as leek, onion and garlic are also very popular. The best-known vegetable of the region is the great Tientsin White Cabbage, a cross between cabbage, lettuce and celery, which is known outside the area as Chinese cabbage. The region also borders the Gulf of Chilli to the east, and here there is a great supply of prawns (shrimps) in the muddy waters

— so there are many prawn (shrimp) dishes, some of which are cooked in their shell.

The cooking of any given area also, of course, reflects its history. Peking has been the capital of China for nearly a thousand years, and the area has been over-run more than once by Tartar invaders from the north, who carried with them the Moslem traditions of Central Asia. Hence the metropolitan tradition which still exists in Peking, originally fostered in the great palace kitchens, where the best provincial dishes were recreated and integrated with one another. Peking cuisine can perhaps still be described today as 'metropolitan mandarin', or metropolitan haute cuisine. And the popular sesame, in all its forms — sesame oil, sesame seeds and sesame paste — brought originally by the Tartar hordes, is now a staple of the north Chinese diet.

Shanghai and East China cooking

Shanghai is China's largest city and one of the two or three largest in the world. It is situated where the Yangtze flows into the East China Sea, and also in the area are the other main cities of the Lower Yangtze, Soochow, Hangchow, Nanking and Yangchow. The cuisine of the area is, however, on the whole less well known than that of Canton or Peking, or even for that matter of Szechuan, probably because it is less distinctive.

The Lower Yangtze is lush with vegetation and fresh water produce. No one eats lamb or mutton here, for the population prefers ducks, chicken, pork and freshwater fish, such as crabs and snails. Gourmets in the area are proud of the 'purity' of their food, and there are many long-cooked or long-simmered dishes, which are 'pure' in that there is only one principal ingredient, and even though some may be supported by several 'supplementary' ingredients, they are not stirred and mixed up with them. In other cases, where the food is dry stir-fried, some of the ingredients (chicken livers and kidneys, or miniature pork chops) are stir-fried, sliced or chopped still in their original state, and they are seasoned only by dipping them into salt and pepper dips before eating. An immense quantity of ducks is produced in this region; several millions of them are dried and 'pressed' in Nanking every year.

Hangchow is justifiably famous for its Soya Duck, and for the fresh succulence of its shrimps, which come from the lakes of this lake city. Steaming as a cooking method is extensively used and many long-cooked meat dishes are 'steamed' in closed receptacles. Some of the best-known stir-fried dishes consist simply of shredded or minced (ground) meat stir-fried with pickles or salted vegetables. There is probably a wider range of vegetables here than in any other part of China, and they are often cooked in conjunction with bean curd. The food on the whole is less saucy than in the south and with a far wider range of vegetables and freshwater produce than in the northern regions of China.

Canton and South China cooking

The climate in south China is semi-tropical, and the coast bordering on the South China Sea is several thousand miles long. Although the area is mountainous (tea grows on the hills), the valleys are fruit-laden, and along the coast fishing has long been an industry. As would be expected, both fruit and seafood — and especially seafood — play an important part in the cooking of the region. Even abroad, where most Chinese restaurants are Cantonese, nearly everyone has heard of such dishes as Cantonese lobster or ginger and onion crab. Cantonese steamed fish is unbeatable. In Fukien they cook their rice-flour noodles with all kinds of seafood, such as oysters, mussels, squid, crab and shrimps (a sort of noodle 'Paella'!) In order to combat the 'fishiness' of seafood and fish, fresh root ginger is widely used, as are salted and dried vegetables, which are either fried in the oil or steamed with the fish and seafood.

Canton is the most populous and prosperous city in the south. Here the affluent community used to take great trouble to make their food extra refined and sophisticated (some would say decadent!). In cooking their suckling pig and frying their pigeons and young chickens, they make the skins crispy. The majority of their stir-fried dishes are saucy and extremely savoury, and many have seafood incorporated, even though the main ingredient is meat (Beef in oyster sauce) (page 90). Fruits often creep into meat dishes, too: so you have Chicken stuffed with sour plums, lichee pork, or the popular sweet and sour sauce which, at its best, should have some fruit juice incorporated into it.

Szechuan and West China cooking

Szechuan is situated over a thousand miles up the Yangtze. Being so far from the sea, much of the food has to be salted, dried, smoked or spiced with chilli to be preserved. When these preserved foods and preserving techniques are employed in cooking, they naturally help to produce a cuisine which is highly distinctive. Szechuan is also a large, enclosed basin walled in by mountains, and the climate in the summer is hot and humid. The Chinese who came from the dry plains of Central China and the arid north must have felt that they needed foods which were hot and spicy to encourage a sweat to counteract the 'chang chi' (jungle dampness) of the region. With all these contributory factors, over the years Szechuan tradition and practice has become well-known throughout China and now, even abroad.

In producing spicy food, Szechuan cooking makes great use of its chilli peppers. When the hotness of the chilli is mixed with the peanut-butter taste of sesame, you have a whole series of dishes called 'Ma La' or hot and sesame; when the hotness of the chilli is added to salted black beans and strong-tasting vegetables, you have a whole series of dishes called 'Yu Hsiang' (or fish-cooking ingredients). The usual Chinese 5-spice combination (star anise, anise pepper, fennel, cloves and cinnamon) seems more frequently used here than in other areas of China. When meat or poultry is stewed, it is often stewed with the addition of dried tangerine peel. When it is smoked, it is often smoked by burning tea and camphorwood as fuel. Red pepper oil (ground red pepper heated in oil and strained) is often used either as a dip, or in stir-fried cooking to produce or induce that 'streak of hot oblivion' so beloved by those who have a genuine appreciation of 'hot' food — and gullets of iron!

Peking and North China cooking

Quick-fried lamb with spring onions (scallions)

Young leeks may be used instead of spring onions (scallions).

METRIC/IMPERIAL	AMERICAN
450 g/1 lb leg of lamb	1 lb leg of lamb
7.5 ml/1½ tsp salt	1½ tsp salt
25 ml/1½ tbsp soya sauce	1½ tbsp soy sauce
25 ml/1½ tbsp cornflour	1½ tbsp cornstarch
60 ml/4 tbsp vegetable oil	4 tbsp vegetable oil
6 spring onions	6 scallions
4 cloves garlic	4 cloves garlic
15 ml/1 tbsp lard	1 tbsp lard
25 ml/1½ tbsp dry sherry	1½ tbsp dry sherry
5 ml/1 tsp sugar	5 ml/1 tsp sugar

To prepare: Cut the lamb into 4 cm/1½ in by 2.5 cm/1 in slices. Rub all over with salt, soya sauce, cornflour (cornstarch) and a quarter of the oil. Leave for 30 minutes. Cut the spring onions (scallions) into 5 cm/2 in lengths. Crush the garlic.
To cook: Heat the remaining oil in a large frying-pan over high heat. When the oil is hot, add the lamb and garlic. Stir-fry for 2 minutes. Add the lard and when it has melted, add the spring onions (scallions), sherry and sugar. Stir-fry for a further 1 minute.
To serve: Turn on to a warmed dish.

Stir-fried giant prawns (Gulf shrimps)

METRIC/IMPERIAL	AMERICAN
450–575 g/1–1¼ lb large prawns in shell (about 8–10)	1–1¼ lb large Gulf shrimps in shell (about 8–10)
15 ml/1 tbsp salt	1 tbsp salt
900 ml/1½ pints water	3¾ cups water
4–5 cloves garlic	4–5 cloves garlic
4 spring onions	4 scallions
45 ml/3 tbsp vegetable oil	3 tbsp vegetable oil
25 ml/1½ tbsp soya sauce	1½ tbsp soy sauce
15 ml/1 tbsp hoisin sauce	1 tbsp hoisin sauce
15 ml/1 tbsp sherry	1 tbsp sherry
7.5 ml/1½ tsp sugar	1½ tsp sugar
15 ml/1 tbsp lard	1 tbsp lard

To prepare: Wash the prawns (shrimps) under cold running water. Dissolve the salt in the water. Soak the prawns (shrimps) in the salted water for 1 hour, and drain. Pat dry on paper towels. Crush the garlic. Cut the spring onions (scallions) into 1 cm/¼ in lengths.
To cook: Heat the oil in a frying-pan over moderate heat. When the oil is hot, add the prawns (shrimps) and three-quarters of the spring onions (scallions) and garlic. Stir-fry for 1 minute. Sprinkle with soya sauce, hoisin sauce, sherry and sugar. Stir-fry until all the sauce in the pan has evaporated, about 1½ minutes. Add the lard and sprinkle with the remaining spring onions (scallions). Stir-fry for a further ½ minute.
To serve: Turn on to a warmed dish. The diner should break off the head, and chew and suck out the meat from the shells. For connoisseurs of prawns (shrimps), prawns (shrimps)-in-shells are considered tastier than those which are shelled before cooking.

Five ingredient soup

METRIC/IMPERIAL	AMERICAN
55 ml/3½ tbsp beche-de-mer	3½ tbsp beche-de-mer
55 ml/3½ tbsp Chinese dried mushrooms	3½ tbsp Chinese dried mushrooms
55 ml/3½ tbsp raw chicken breast	3½ tbsp raw chicken breast
55 ml/3½ tbsp smoked ham	3½ tbsp smoked ham
55 ml/3½ tbsp bamboo shoot	3½ tbsp bamboo shoot
900 ml/1½ pints clear broth (page 25)	3¾ cups clear broth (page 25)
1 chicken stock cube	1 chicken stock cube
30 ml/2 tbsp soya sauce	2 tbsp soy sauce
45 ml/3 tbsp wine vinegar	3 tbsp wine vinegar
pepper	pepper
20 ml/1¼ tbsp cornflour, mixed with 60 ml/4 tbsp water	1¼ tbsp cornstarch, mixed with 4 tbsp water
15 ml/1 tbsp lard or chicken fat	1 tbsp lard or chicken fat
15 ml/1 tbsp chopped coriander or parsley	1 tbsp chopped coriander or parsley

To prepare: Soak the beche-de-mer in water for 3 days, drain and cut into small cubes. Soak the dried mushrooms in 300 ml/½ pint (1¼ cups) of water for 30 minutes. Remove the stalks and cut the caps into small pieces. Cut the chicken meat, ham and bamboo shoot into similar-sized pieces.
To cook: Heat the broth in a saucepan. When it boils, add the 'five ingredients' and the crumbled stock cube. Simmer gently for 15 minutes. Add the soya sauce, vinegar and pepper, and stir in the cornflour (cornstarch) mixture. When the mixture comes to the boil again, add the lard or chicken fat. Sprinkle with chopped coriander or parsley. Bring to the boil and remove from the heat.
To serve: Pour into warmed bowls, or a large tureen.

Peking duck

METRIC/IMPERIAL	AMERICAN
1 × 2 kg/4 lb duck	1 × 4 lb duck
15 ml/1 tbsp malt sugar or barley sugar	1 tbsp malt sugar or barley sugar
15 ml/1 tbsp soya sauce	1 tbsp soy sauce
300 ml/½ pint water	1¼ cups water

Pancake filling

METRIC/IMPERIAL	AMERICAN
4–5 spring onions	4–5 scallions
½ medium-sized cucumber	½ medium-sized cucumber

Sauce

METRIC/IMPERIAL	AMERICAN
30 ml/2 tbsp soya sauce	2 tbsp soy sauce
20 ml/1¼ tbsp soya paste	1¼ tbsp soy paste
20 ml/1¼ tbsp hoisin sauce	1¼ tbsp hoisin sauce
20 ml/1¼ tbsp sugar	1¼ tbsp sugar
30 ml/2 tbsp plum sauce	2 tbsp plum sauce
15 ml/1 tbsp sesame oil	1 tbsp sesame oil

To prepare: Clean the duck under cold running water, then douse the skin with a large kettleful of boiling water, turning the bird over once. Shake and pat the skin with paper towels. Hang the duck up by the neck to dry overnight in an airy place. Combine the malt sugar, soya sauce and water until they are well blended. Brush the duck with this mixture. Leave to dry for 30 minutes. Cut the spring onions (scallions) into 5 cm/2 in lengths. Shred the cucumber. Combine all the sauce ingredients until they are well blended.

To cook: Put the duck on a rack in a roasting pan. Put the pan into the oven preheated to 190°C (375°F) Gas Mark 5. Roast for 1 hour, without basting or opening the oven. After 1 hour of roasting, the duck should be sufficiently cooked and the skin crispy. Put the sauce mixture into a saucepan and cook for 2 minutes, stirring constantly.

To serve: Carve the skin of the duck into approximately 4 cm/1½ in by 2.5 cm/1 in pieces and spread out on a warmed dish. Carve the meat of the duck into similar-sized slices and place on a separate warmed dish. The duck should be eaten by inserting one or two pieces of skin and duck into a pancake and rolling up. Brush the pancake with 7.5 ml/½ tbsp of sauce and accompany with a large pinch or two of shredded cucumber and spring onions (scallions). The aim is to achieve a 'triple contrast' in texture: crackling skin, succulent duck meat and crunchy vegetables. This is enough for six to eight people, with other dishes.

Pancakes

The pancakes for Peking Duck can either be bought from Chinese food stores or supermarkets where they are usually available nowadays, or made in the following way:

METRIC/IMPERIAL	AMERICAN
225 g/½ lb plain flour	2 cups all-purpose flour
250 ml/8 fl oz boiling water	1 cup boiling water
30 ml/2 tbsp sesame oil	2 tbsp sesame oil

To prepare: Sift the flour into a bowl. Slowly pour the boiling water on to the flour, beating constantly with a wooden spoon until the mixture forms a dough. Knead the dough for 5–6 minutes, then 'rest' for 10 minutes. Form the dough into a long roll of about 5 cm/2 in in diameter. Cut the roll into 1.5 cm/½ in slices. Roll the slices into 15 cm/6 in diameter pancakes. Brush the top of two pancakes with sesame oil and place one pancake on top of another, the oiled sides facing each other. Sandwich the remaining pancakes in the same way.

To cook: Place a heavy, ungreased frying-pan over moderate heat. When it is hot, place a double-pancake on the ungreased pan and heat for approximately 3 minutes on each side (some brown spots will appear and some parts of the pancakes will start to bubble, when it is cooked). When this happens, remove the pancake from the pan and cool a little. Pull the pancakes apart into two. Fold each one across the centre, on the greased side. Stack on a heatproof dish and place in a steamer. Steam for 10 minutes. (These pancakes will keep in the refrigerator for 2–3 days, and should be steamed again for 7–8 minutes if they are to be kept for any length of time before serving.) Makes about ten to twelve pancakes.

'Oil poached' fish in Peking wine sauce

METRIC/IMPERIAL	AMERICAN
30–45 ml/2–3 tbsp wood ears	2–3 tbsp wood ears
450 g/1 lb fish fillets (sole, bream, halibut, carp, etc)	1 lb fish fillets (sole, bream, halibut, carp, etc)
7.5 ml/1½ tsp salt	1½ tsp salt
1 egg white	1 egg white
20 ml/1¼ tbsp cornflour	1¼ tbsp cornstarch
3 slices root ginger	3 slices root ginger
vegetable oil for deep-frying	vegetable oil for deep-frying
30 ml/2 tbsp lard	2 tbsp lard

Sauce

10 ml/2 tsp cornflour, mixed with 60 ml/4 tbsp water	2 tsp cornstarch, mixed with 4 tbsp water
45 ml/3 tbsp clear broth (page 25)	3 tbsp clear broth (page 25)
60 ml/4 tbsp white wine	4 tbsp white wine
7.5 ml/1½ tsp sugar	1½ tsp sugar
2.5 ml/½ tsp salt	½ tsp salt

To prepare: Soak the dried fungi in water for 30 minutes. Drain, then pat dry. Cut the fish into 5 cm/2 in by 2.5 cm/1 in slices. Rub all over with the salt, and leave for 30 minutes. Coat with the egg white and cornflour (cornstarch). Peel and chop the ginger. Combine all the sauce ingredients until they are well blended.

To cook: Heat the oil in a deep-frying pan until it is very hot. Remove from the heat to cool for ¾ minute. Using a slotted spoon, lower one or two pieces of fish at a time into the oil to 'poach' for 1 minute. Set the pan over moderate heat for 1 minute. Remove the fish from the oil and drain on paper towels. Heat the fat in a frying-pan over moderate heat. When the fat has melted, add the ginger and wood ears. Stir-fry for 1 minute. Remove the ginger. Pour in the sauce mixture and stir until it thickens. Reduce the heat to low. Add the drained fish pieces to the sauce, one by one, in a single layer. Poach them in the sauce for 1–1½ minutes.

To serve: Arrange the fish mixture on a warmed dish, so that it contrasts well with the blackness of the wood ears. Pour the remaining thickened sauce over the fish.

Peking duck

85

Shanghai and East China cooking

Plain shallow-fried pork chops with salt and pepper dip

METRIC/IMPERIAL	AMERICAN
700 g/1 ½ lb pork chops	1½ lb pork chops
75–90 ml/5–6 tbsp vegetable oil	5–6 tbsp vegetable oil

Dip

45–60 ml/3–4 tbsp salt	3–4 tbsp salt
5 ml/1 tsp black pepper (freshly ground if possible)	1 tsp black pepper (freshly ground if possible)

To prepare: Chop each pork chop through the bone into 4 pieces. Rub all over with 15 ml/1 tbsp of the oil. Prepare the dip by mixing the salt and pepper in a small dry frying-pan over low heat. Cook the mixture for about 1½–2 minutes, stirring constantly, until a distinct bouquet rises from the mixture. Transfer the mixture to two small dishes and arrange them on the dining table.

To cook: Heat the remaining oil in a frying-pan over high heat. When the oil is very hot, add the pork chop pieces. Stir-fry them for 6 minutes, until they become browned. Remove from the pan with a slotted spoon.

To serve: Arrange the pork on a warmed dish, beside the dip dishes. The diners should dip the pork pieces into the dip before eating.

Quick-fried shrimps with cucumber

METRIC/IMPERIAL	AMERICAN
225–350 g/½–¾ lb shrimps	½–¾ lb shrimps
5 ml/1 tsp salt	1 tsp salt
55 ml/3½ tbsp vegetable oil	3½ tbsp vegetable oil
½ medium-sized cucumber	½ medium-sized cucumber
25 ml/1½ tbsp soya sauce	1½ tbsp soy sauce
7.5 ml/1½ tsp sugar	1½ tsp sugar
30 ml/2 tbsp clear broth (page 25)	2 tbsp clear broth (page 25)
30 ml/2 tbsp sherry	2 tbsp sherry

To prepare: Rub the shrimps with the salt and 10 ml/2 tsp of oil. Leave for 15 minutes. Dice the cucumber into small cubes.

To cook: Heat the remaining oil in a frying-pan over high heat. When the oil is very hot, add the shrimps. Stir-fry for ½ minute. Add the cucumber. Sprinkle with soya sauce, sugar, broth and sherry. Stir-fry for a further 1½ minutes.

To serve: Turn on to a warmed dish.

Ham with lotus seeds in honey sauce

METRIC/IMPERIAL	AMERICAN
1 × 5 cm/2 in thick slice of ham (about 1–1 ¼ kg/2–2 ½ lb)	1 × 2 in thick slice of ham (about 2–2 ½ lb)
45 ml/3 tbsp brown sugar	3 tbsp brown sugar
1.5 ml/¼ tsp ground cinnamon	¼ tsp ground cinnamon
90 ml/6 tbsp water	6 tbsp water
300 ml/½ pint lotus seeds or peanuts	1 ⅔ cups lotus seeds or peanuts

Honey sauce

45 ml/3 tbsp clear honey	3 tbsp clear honey
25 ml/1½ tbsp sugar	1½ tbsp sugar
10 ml/2 tsp cornflour, mixed with 45 ml/3 tbsp water	2 tsp cornstarch, mixed with 3 tbsp water

To prepare: Put the ham, in one piece, on a heatproof dish. Put into a steamer and steam steadily for 1 hour (or improvise by placing the dish on a bowl turned upside down in a large saucepan with a 2.5 cm/1 in layer of boiling water, and boil for 1 hour). Cut the ham vertically into 8 pieces, then reassemble them into the original shape. Put the brown sugar, cinnamon and water into a small saucepan. Heat until the sugar has dissolved. Add the lotus seeds and stir and turn in the syrup for 2 minutes. Combine all the sauce ingredients until they are well blended.

To cook: Spoon the lotus seed and syrup mixture over the ham. Return the dish to the steamer and steam steadily for a further 1½ hours. Put the sauce mixture into a small saucepan and cook, stirring constantly, until it thickens.

To serve: Pour the sauce over the lotus seeds and ham. After 2½ hours of steaming the ham should be tender enough to be broken into small bite-sized pieces with chopsticks. Serves four to six.

Ham with lotus seeds in honey sauce

Quick-braised heart of green cabbage

METRIC/IMPERIAL	AMERICAN
700 g/1 1/2 lb small green cabbage	6 cups cabbage
3 cloves garlic	3 cloves garlic
55 ml/3 1/2 tbsp vegetable oil	3 1/2 tbsp vegetable oil
10 ml/2 tsp salt	2 tsp salt
1/2 chicken stock cube	1/2 chicken stock cube
60 ml/4 tbsp clear broth (page 25)	4 tbsp clear broth (page 25)
15 ml/1 tbsp lard	1 tbsp lard

To prepare: Discard any coarse or discoloured outer leaves from the cabbage. Cut the heart into quarters or sixes. Clean thoroughly and pat dry. Crush the garlic.

To cook: Heat the oil in a saucepan over moderate heat. When the oil is hot, add the greens. Stir-fry for 1 1/2 minutes, until every leaf is well coated. Sprinkle with the salt, garlic, crumbled stock cube and broth. Stir and turn a few times. Cook for 3–4 minutes. Add the lard and stir and turn a few times.

To serve: Turn on to a warmed dish. This dish when cooked is an exceptionally pretty jade colour, and it makes an excellent accompaniment to rich brown soya-braised meat dishes.

Braised fish with bean curd

METRIC/IMPERIAL	AMERICAN
1 × 1 kg/2 lb whole fish (carp, mullet, bream, mackerel, etc)	1 × 2 lb whole fish, (carp, mullet, bream, mackerel, etc)
30 ml/2 tbsp flour	2 tbsp flour
1 medium-sized onion	1 medium-sized onion
3 spring onions	3 scallions
2 cakes bean curd	2 cakes bean curd
30 ml/2 tbsp snow pickles, or any salted pickles	2 tbsp snow pickles, or any salted pickles
75 ml/5 tbsp vegetable oil	5 tbsp vegetable oil
300 ml/1/2 pint clear broth (page 25)	1 1/4 cups clear broth (page 25)
45 ml/3 tbsp soya sauce	3 tbsp soy sauce
7.5 ml/1 1/2 tsp sugar	1 1/2 tsp sugar
30 ml/2 tbsp sherry	2 tbsp sherry
15 ml/1 tbsp lard	1 tbsp lard
pepper	pepper

To prepare: Clean and gut the fish thoroughly, then chop the fish into fairly large pieces. Rub all over with the flour. Slice the onion thinly. Cut the spring onions (scallions) into 2.5 cm/1 in lengths. Dice each bean curd cake into a dozen pieces. Chop the pickles.

To cook: Heat the oil in a large frying-pan over high heat. When the oil is hot, add the onion and pickles and stir-fry for 1 minute. Add the fish and turn the pieces in the oil for 3–4 minutes. Pour off any excess oil. Pour in the broth, soya sauce, sugar and sherry. Stir-fry the fish in the sauce for 2 minutes. Remove the fish pieces from the pan. Add the bean curd, lard and pepper and cook in the soup for 5 minutes. Return the fish to the pan and sprinkle with the spring onions (scallions). Turn the contents over a few times. Reduce the heat to moderately low and simmer for 2–3 minutes.

To serve: Turn into a deep-sided, warmed dish, or large bowl. This is a very popular winter dish in Shanghai. It is excellent with rice. Serves four to six.

Canton and South China cooking

Cantonese roast duck

METRIC/IMPERIAL	AMERICAN
1 × 2 kg/4 lb duck	1 × 4 lb duck

Filling

3 cloves garlic	3 cloves garlic
1 medium-sized onion	1 medium-sized onion
2.5 ml/1/2 tsp 5-spice powder	1/2 tsp 5-spice powder
10 ml/2 tsp sugar	2 tsp sugar
75 ml/5 tbsp clear broth (page 25)	5 tbsp clear broth (page 25)
25 ml/1 1/2 tbsp soya sauce	1 1/2 tbsp soy sauce
25 ml/1 1/2 tbsp soya paste	1 1/2 tbsp soy paste
45 ml/3 tbsp sherry	3 tbsp sherry

Skin coating

300 ml/1/2 pint water	1 1/4 cups water
60–75 ml/4–5 tbsp clear honey	4–5 tbsp clear honey
75 ml/5 tbsp wine vinegar	5 tbsp wine vinegar
30 ml/2 tbsp soya sauce	2 tbsp soy sauce

To prepare: Clean the duck under cold running water. Crush the garlic. Slice the onion very thinly. Combine the garlic, onion, 5-spice powder, sugar, broth, soya sauce, soya paste and sherry until they are well blended. Spoon the mixture into the cavity of the duck and close with skewers or a trussing needle and thread. Combine the coating ingredients until they are well blended. Put them into a small saucepan and heat until the honey has dissolved. Douse the skin of the duck with a kettleful of boiling water, turning the bird over once. Shake and pat dry with paper towels. Hang the duck up by the neck to dry for 1 hour in an airy spot. Brush the duck with the coating mixture and hang up to dry for the second time, this time overnight.

To cook: Put the duck on a rack in a roasting pan and put the pan into the oven preheated to 220°C (425°F) Gas Mark 7. Roast for 10 minutes. Turn the duck over and roast for a further 10 minutes. Reduce the temperature to 190°C (375°F) Gas Mark 5. Turn the duck over once more and roast for 40 minutes. Increase the temperature to 200°C (400°F) Gas Mark 6. Brush once more with the coating mixture and roast for a final 10 minutes.

To serve: Chop the duck neatly into bite-sized pieces and serve hot or cold. This liquid from the cavity of the duck can be used as a gravy. This will serve four people substantially.

Cantonese roast duck

Beef in oyster sauce with broccoli

METRIC/IMPERIAL	AMERICAN
450 g/1 lb rump or fillet of beef	1 lb rump or fillet of beef
5 ml/1 tsp salt	1 tsp salt
15 ml/1 tbsp soya sauce	1 tbsp soy sauce
25 ml/1½ tbsp cornflour	1½ tbsp cornstarch
60 ml/4 tbsp vegetable oil	4 tbsp vegetable oil
30 ml/2 tbsp oyster sauce	2 tbsp oyster sauce

Broccoli	**Broccoli**
225–350 g/½–¾ lb broccoli	1½–2 cups broccoli
150 ml/¼ pint clear broth (page 25)	⅝ cup clear broth (page 25)
5 ml/1 tsp salt	1 tsp salt
15 ml/1 tbsp lard	1 tbsp lard

To prepare: Cut the beef into 5 cm/2 in by 2.5 cm/1 in slices. Rub all over with the salt, soya sauce, cornflour (cornstarch) and a quarter of the oil. Leave for 15 minutes. Break the broccoli into small individual flowerets.

To cook: Heat the broth, salt and lard in a saucepan over moderate heat. When the mixture boils, add the broccoli. Cook, turning occasionally, for 7–8 minutes, until the liquid in the pan has almost evaporated. Heat the remaining oil in a frying-pan over high heat. When the oil is hot, add the beef. Stir-fry for 1½ minutes. Add the oyster sauce and stir-fry for a further 1 minute.

To serve: Turn on to a warmed dish, spreading the broccoli on the bottom and covering with the beef.

Poached shrimps served with dips

METRIC/IMPERIAL	AMERICAN
700 g/1½ lb shrimps in shell	1½ lb shrimps in shell
15 ml/1 tbsp salt	1 tbsp salt
600 ml/1 pint water	2½ cups water

Dip 1	**Dip 1**
45–60 ml/3–4 tbsp hoisin sauce	3–4 tbsp hoisin sauce

Dip 2	**Dip 2**
30 ml/2 tbsp soya sauce	2 tbsp soy sauce
45 ml/3 tbsp wine vinegar, or Chinese aromatic vinegar	3 tbsp wine vinegar, or Chinese aromatic vinegar
4 slices root ginger, peeled and shredded	4 slices root ginger, peeled and shredded

Dip 3	**Dip 3**
30 ml/2 tbsp soya sauce	2 tbsp soy sauce
40 ml/2½ tbsp wine vinegar, or Chinese aromatic vinegar	2½ tbsp wine vinegar, or Chinese aromatic vinegar
4 cloves garlic, crushed	4 cloves garlic, crushed
2 spring onions, chopped	2 scallions, chopped
15 ml/1 tbsp sesame oil	1 tbsp sesame oil

Dip 4	**Dip 4**
45 ml/3 tbsp soya sauce	3 tbsp soy sauce
15 ml/1 tbsp chilli sauce	1 tbsp chilli sauce

To prepare: Wash the shrimps under cold running water. Dissolve the salt in the water. Soak the shrimps in the salted water for 45 minutes, and drain. Pat dry on paper towels.

Prepare all of the individual dips by mixing the ingredients together until they are well blended.

To cook: Heat a large saucepan of water over moderate heat. Bring to the boil and add the shrimps. When the water comes to the boil again, turn off the heat and leave the shrimps for 3 minutes. Drain.

To serve: Transfer the shrimps to a large bowl and surround with bowls containing the dips. To eat, use your fingers to break off the heads of the shrimps and dip the exposed part of the meat in one of the dips. Eat by nibbling out the rest of the meat from the shells, by biting from back to front. When the shrimps are really fresh, the southern Chinese feel that poaching is the best way to cook them.

Cantonese ginger and onion crab

METRIC/IMPERIAL	AMERICAN
2–3 medium-sized crabs	2–3 medium-sized crabs
4 slices root ginger	4 slices root ginger
3–4 cloves garlic	3–4 cloves garlic
10 ml/2 tsp salt	2 tsp salt
2–3 medium-sized onions	2–3 medium-sized onions
3 spring onions	3 scallions
60 ml/4 tbsp vegetable oil	4 tbsp vegetable oil
60 ml/4 tbsp clear broth (page 25)	4 tbsp clear broth (page 25)
25 ml/1½ tbsp soya sauce	1½ tbsp soy sauce
60 ml/4 tbsp dry sherry	4 tbsp dry sherry

To prepare: Separate the large main shell from the body of each crab by inserting a knife under the shell as a lever. Crack the claws and shells. Chop the bodies into quarters or sixes (leaving a leg or two attached to use as a 'handle' when eating). Scrape and remove all the spongy parts. Peel and shred the ginger, and crush the garlic. Sprinkle the crab with the salt, ginger, and garlic. Slice the onions thinly. Cut the spring onions (scallions) into 2.5 cm/1 in lengths.

To cook: Heat the oil in a deep frying-pan over high heat. When the oil is very hot, add the onions. Stir-fry for 1½ minutes. Add the crab pieces and stir-fry for 2½ minutes. Add the broth, soya sauce and sherry. Cover the pan and cook for 2 minutes. Uncover and sprinkle with the spring onions (scallions). Stir-fry for a further 1 minute.

To serve: Turn on to a large, warmed dish.

Double-cooked pork

Szechuan and West China cooking

Double-cooked pork

METRIC/IMPERIAL	AMERICAN
25 ml/1½ tbsp wood ears	1½ tbsp wood ears
700 g/1½ lb belly of pork	1½ lb belly of pork
2 dried chilli peppers, or 10 ml/2 tsp chilli sauce	2 dried chilli peppers or 2 tsp chilli sauce
4 spring onions	4 scallions
4 cloves garlic	4 cloves garlic
55 ml/3½ tbsp vegetable oil	3½ tbsp vegetable oil
15 ml/1 tbsp soya paste	1½ tbsp soy paste
30 ml/2 tbsp soya sauce	2 tbsp soy sauce
15 ml/1 tbsp hoisin sauce, or sweet bean paste	1 tbsp hoisin sauce, or sweet bean paste
30 ml/2 tbsp tomato purée	2 tbsp tomato paste
10 ml/2 tsp sugar	2 tsp sugar
45 ml/3 tbsp clear broth (page 25)	3 tbsp clear broth (page 25)
25 ml/1½ tbsp sherry	1½ tbsp sherry
15 ml/1 tbsp sesame oil	1 tbsp sesame oil

To prepare: Soak the wood ears in water for about 30 minutes. Rinse and drain. Put the pork into a saucepan of boiling water. Bring to the boil and simmer for 25 minutes. Leave to cool. When it is cool, cut, through the fat and skin, into 5 cm/2 in by 4 cm/1½ in slices. Cut the peppers into thin slices, discarding the pips. Cut the spring onions (scallions) into 4 cm/1½ in lengths. Crush the garlic.

To cook: Heat the oil in a frying-pan over moderate heat. When the oil is hot, add the chilli peppers and wood ears, and stir-fry for 1 minute. Add the garlic, soya paste, soya sauce, hoisin sauce, tomato purée (paste), sugar and broth. Stir for ½ minute, until the mixture becomes smooth. Add the pork pieces to the sauce and spread out in one layer. Increase the heat to high and stir and turn the pork in the sauce until it is well coated, and the sauce begins to thicken. Sprinkle with spring onions (scallions), sherry and sesame oil. Stir and turn a few more times.

To serve: Turn on to a warmed dish.

Hot ma po mashed bean curd with minced (ground) beef

METRIC/IMPERIAL	AMERICAN
5–6 medium-sized Chinese dried mushrooms	5–6 medium-sized Chinese dried mushrooms
10 ml/2 tsp salted black beans	2 tsp salted black beans
4 cloves garlic	4 cloves garlic
3 spring onions	3 scallions
2–3 cakes bean curd	2–3 cakes bean curd
60 ml/4 tbsp vegetable oil	4 tbsp vegetable oil
75–90 ml/5–6 tbsp minced beef	5–6 tbsp ground beef
30 ml/2 tbsp soya sauce	2 tbsp soy sauce
30 ml/2 tbsp hoisin sauce	2 tbsp hoisin sauce
10 ml/2 tsp chilli sauce	2 tsp chilli sauce
5 ml/1 tsp sugar	1 tsp sugar
60 ml/4 tbsp clear broth (page 25)	4 tbsp clear broth (page 25)
10 ml/2 tsp cornflour, mixed with 45 ml/3 tbsp water	2 tsp cornstarch, mixed with 3 tbsp water
15 ml/1 tbsp sesame oil	1 tbsp sesame oil

To prepare: Soak the mushrooms in 300 ml/½ pint (1¼ cups) of water for 30 minutes. Soak the black beans in water for 15 minutes. Discard the stalks from the mushrooms and cut the caps into quarters. Reserve the mushroom soaking liquid. Crush the garlic, and cut the spring onions (scallions) into thin rounds. Dice the bean curd cakes into small cubes.

To cook: Heat the oil in a large frying-pan over moderate heat. When the oil is hot, add the black beans. Stir and turn in the oil for ¼ minute. Add the beef, half the spring onions (scallions) and the mushrooms. Stir-fry for 3–4 minutes, until they are well mixed. Add the garlic, 45–60 ml/3–4 tbsp of the mushroom water, the soya sauce, hoisin sauce, chilli sauce, sugar, bean curd and broth. Increase the heat to high and stir-fry the mixture until it comes to the boil. Simmer for 3–4 minutes. Sprinkle with the cornflour (cornstarch) mixture, the remaining spring onions (scallions) and the sesame oil and stir and turn a few more times.

To serve: Turn into a large, warmed flat bowl or deep-sided bowl. This is an excellent dish to accompany rice.

Steamed chicken pudding

METRIC/IMPERIAL	AMERICAN
1 × 1½–2 kg/3–4 lb chicken	1 × 3–4 lb chicken
2 medium-sized onions	2 medium-sized onions
3 slices root ginger	3 slices root ginger
3–4 dried chilli peppers	3–4 dried chilli peppers
450 g/1 lb sweet potatoes or yams	1 lb sweet potatoes or yams
10 ml/2 tsp salt	2 tsp salt

Sauce	Sauce
75–90 ml/5–6 tbsp chicken stock	5–6 tbsp chicken stock
30 ml/2 tbsp soya sauce	2 tbsp soy sauce
30 ml/2 tbsp sherry	2 tbsp sherry
15 ml/1 tbsp cornflour, mixed with 45 m/3 tbsp water	1 tbsp cornstarch, mixed with 3 tbsp water
½ chicken stock cube	½ chicken stock cube
10 ml/2 tsp sesame oil	2 tsp sesame oil

To prepare: Cut the chicken into serving pieces. Cut each leg and wing into three and the body into 8–10 pieces. Put the pieces into a saucepan and just cover with water. Bring to the boil and simmer for 30–35 minutes. Slice the onions thinly. Peel and shred the ginger and shred the pepper (discarding the pips). Cut the sweet potatoes into pieces the same size as the chicken. Combine all the sauce ingredients until they are well blended.

To cook: Sprinkle the chicken pieces with salt and arrange them, skin side down, in a deep heatproof bowl or basin. Pack the sweet potatoes loosely on top. Sprinkle with the ginger, pepper, onion and 30–45 ml/2–3 tbsp of chicken stock. Cover the top with foil and place the basin in a steamer. Steam steadily for 1½ hours. When the chicken and sweet potatoes are ready, heat the sauce mixture in a small saucepan, stirring until it begins to thicken.

To serve: Turn the contents of the basin on to a large, warmed dish. Pour over the sauce. This is one of Szechuan's 'dishes of the people'.

Quick-fried liver with 'fish ingredients'

METRIC/IMPERIAL	AMERICAN
450–575 g/1–1¼ lb pig's liver	1–1¼ lb pig's liver
7.5 ml/1½ tsp salt	1½ tsp salt
15 ml/1 tbsp sherry	1 tbsp sherry
10 ml/2 tsp vegetable oil	2 tsp vegetable oil
15 ml/1 tbsp cornflour, mixed with 30 ml/2 tbsp water	1 tbsp cornstarch, mixed with 2 tbsp water
10 ml/2 tsp garlic	2 tsp garlic
10 ml/2 tsp ginger	2 tsp ginger
20 ml/1¼ tbsp spring onions	1¼ tbsp scallions
45 ml/3 tbsp lard	3 tbsp lard

Sauce	Sauce
15 ml/1 tbsp sherry	1 tbsp sherry
25 ml/1½ tbsp soya sauce	1½ tbsp soy sauce
25 ml/1½ tbsp tomato purée	1½ tbsp tomato paste
25 ml/1½ tbsp wine vinegar	1½ tbsp wine vinegar
25 ml/1½ tbsp clear broth (page 25)	1½ tbsp clear broth (page 25)
7.5 ml/1½ tsp sugar	1½ tsp sugar

To prepare: Cut the liver into 5 cm/2 in by 2.5 cm/1 in slices. Rub all over with salt, sherry, oil and the cornflour (cornstarch) mixture. Leave for 15 minutes. Crush the garlic, peel and chop the ginger. Chop the spring onions (scallions). Combine all the sauce ingredients until they are well blended.

To cook: Heat the lard in a frying-pan over moderate heat. When the fat has melted, add the liver, spreading out the pieces in one layer. Increase the heat to high and stir-fry for 15 seconds. Sprinkle with the ginger, garlic and spring onions (scallions) and stir-fry for ½ minute. Pour the sauce mixture into the pan. When the mixture comes to the boil, stir-fry for a further ½ minute.

To serve: Turn on to a warmed dish. 'Fish Ingredients' — ginger, garlic, onion, vinegar, soya sauce (or salted black beans) — the ingredients customarily associated with the cooking of fish — are applied to a whole range of Szechuan meat dishes.

Quick-fried chilli-hot kidneys

METRIC/IMPERIAL	AMERICAN
350–450 g/¾–1 lb pig's kidney	¾–1 lb pig's kidney
7.5 ml/1½ tsp salt	1½ tsp salt
25 ml/1½ tbsp sherry	1½ tbsp sherry
30 ml/2 tbsp vegetable oil	2 tbsp vegetable oil
2 cloves garlic	2 cloves garlic
3 slices root ginger	3 slices root ginger
3 spring onions	3 scallions
2 dried chilli peppers	2 dried chilli peppers
1 red pepper	1 red pepper
7.5 ml/1½ tsp sugar	1½ tsp sugar
25 ml/1½ tbsp wine vinegar	1½ tbsp wine vinegar
25 ml/1½ tbsp soya sauce	1½ tbsp soy sauce
25 ml/1½ tbsp clear broth (page 25)	1½ tbsp clear broth (page 25)
5 ml/1 tsp chilli sauce	1 tsp chilli sauce
10 ml/2 tsp cornflour, mixed with 30 ml/2 tbsp water	2 tsp cornstarch, mixed with 2 tbsp water
45 ml/3 tbsp lard	3 tbsp lard

To prepare: Remove the membrane and gristle, then cut each kidney into half. Cut a dozen criss-cross cuts over the surface and halfway through the pieces. Cut again into thin strips. Rub all over with the salt, sherry and a quarter of the oil. Crush the garlic and peel and chop the ginger. Cut the spring onions (scallions) into 2.5 cm/1 in lengths. Finely chop the chilli peppers, discarding the pips. Remove the pith and seeds from the pepper and cut into 1.5 cm/½ in slices. Combine the sugar, vinegar, soya sauce, broth, chilli sauce and cornflour (cornstarch) mixture until they are well blended.

To cook: Heat the lard and the remaining oil in a frying-pan over high heat. When the fat has melted, add the kidney pieces. Stir-fry them for 15–18 seconds, then remove with a slotted spoon. Add the chilli peppers. Stir-fry for 10 seconds. Add the ginger, garlic and spring onions (scallions). Stir-fry for 10 seconds. Return the kidney pieces to the pan, and add the pepper. Stir and turn a few times, then pour the sauce mixture into the pan. Stir-fry for 15 seconds.

To serve: Turn on to a warmed dish. When the dish is cooked, the kidney should be cooked through but still crisp and crunchy to taste.

Szechuan hot pot

The Chinese hot pot is the eastern equivalent to a fondue. The special hot pot, as it is called (page 80, far left), is filled and set over a spirit burner then diners help themselves with chopsticks or spoons. If a hot pot is unobtainable, improvise by placing a casserole on top of the spirit burner.

METRIC/IMPERIAL	AMERICAN
75 g/3 oz raw chicken breast	3 oz raw chicken breast
2 chicken livers	2 chicken livers
75 g/3 oz pig's kidney	3 oz pig's kidney
75 g/3 oz raw lean beef	3 oz raw lean beef
125 g/4 oz raw white fish	4 oz raw white fish
75 g/3 oz white or Chinese cabbage	3 oz white or Chinese cabbage
125 g/4 oz spinach	4 oz spinach
30 ml/2 tbsp vegetable oil	2 tbsp vegetable oil
50 g/2 oz shelled peanuts	2 oz shelled peanuts
2 medium-sized gherkins	2 medium-sized gherkins
1 cake bean curd	1 cake bean curd
1¼ L/2 pints hot clear broth (page 25)	5 cups hot clear broth (page 25)
salt and pepper	salt and pepper
30 ml/2 tbsp coriander leaves	2 tbsp coriander leaves
croûtons	croûtons

To prepare: Cut the chicken, chicken livers, kidney, beef, fish and cabbage into small, matchstick strips. Wash and chop the spinach. Heat the oil until very hot and fry the peanuts for 3 minutes, then drain. Cut the gherkins into very thin strips. Cut the bean curd into 12 pieces.

To cook and serve: Pour the hot clear broth into a hot pot (or casserole) and take to the table. Place the pot over a lighted spirit burner. When the broth comes to the boil, add the cabbage. Cook for 1 minute, then add the chicken, chicken livers, kidney, beef, spinach, gherkins, bean curd and seasoning. Bring to the boil again, and add the fish and coriander. Finally add the peanuts and croûtons. When the mixture comes to the boil again, the hot pot is ready.

This is a winter dish (regarded as a 'large soup main dish') which is drunk and eaten throughout the meal in conjunction with other dishes. It is served at a family dinner, rather than a banquet.

Index

Acknowledgements

The publishers wish to thank the following individuals and organizations for their kind permission to reproduce the photographs in this book:

Bryce Attwell 36, 59, 72; Barry Bullough 68–69, 78; Fruit Producers' Council 78–79; Melvin Grey 1, 2–3, 4–5, 10–11, 13, 14, 15, 17, 18–19, 21, 22–23, 24, 26–27, 32–33, 35, 39, 41, 42 above, 42–43, 44, 45, 49, 50–51, 53, 54, 54–55, 63, 64, 65, 67, 68 left, 70, 71, 73, 74, 75, 76, 77, 80–81, 84–85, 87, 89, 91, 93; Sonia Halliday endpapers; John Lee 29, 37, 46, 52, 58; Neil Lorimer 40, 57, 60; Paul Kemp 30, 61, 94.

The publishers would like to thank the following sources for the loan of accessories for photography:
Craftsmen Potters Association of Great Britain
Inside Outside Shop at Harvey Nichols, Knightsbridge